Pi Profits

How a Tiny Board Can Create Massive Revenue Streams!

By

Gary Covella, Ph.D.

PI PROFITS: HOW A TINY BOARD CAN CREATE MASSIVE REVENUE STREAMS!

First Edition. Oct 2023.
Copyright © Gary Covella
Written by Gary Covella, Ph.D.

CHAPTER 1: INTRODUCTION TO RASPBERRY PI AND OTHER SINGLE BOARD COMPUTERS

Welcome aboard, my friend! As we set sail on this journey of discovery, let me introduce you to a little powerhouse that's causing shockwaves in the entrepreneurial landscape – the Raspberry Pi and other Single Board Computers (SBCs). Now these aren't your traditional computers, no sir! These humble boards, no bigger than your wallet, pack a punch like no other. From smart home automation to bespoke gaming consoles, with these mighty minis, the possibilities are as vast as your imagination.

But it doesn't stop at just fun and games. These tiny titans are a gold mine of profit-making opportunities. You heard it right, they're more than just circuitry and silicon; they're a ticket

Gary Covella, Ph.D.

to a world where your creativity can actually pay your bills. Teachers, artists, tech enthusiasts – lend me your ears! No matter your skill level or background, these pint-sized powerhouses are ready to turn your innovative ideas into reality, and more importantly, into prosperous income streams.

So buckle up, as we dive into the realm of the Raspberry Pi and other SBCs, exploring the many ways you can leverage these tiny tech marvels to earn a pretty penny. Trust me, by the end of this chapter, you'll see these little gizmos not just as computers, but as your new business partners. Let's dive in!

Origins and Evolution of Single Board Computing

Ah, a history lesson, you ask? Well, strap in, because the origins of Single Board Computers (SBCs) like our miraculous Raspberry Pi, are as fascinating as their capabilities. It all started back in the 1970s, with the birth of microprocessors. The first single-board system was none other than the dyna-mic duo of the "Dynabook" computer, an idea by Alan Kay, and Wally Feurzeig's "LOGO" programming language.

2.

Pi Profits

Fast forward to the 1980s, and we were introduced to computers like the BBC Micro and the ZX Spectrum – small, affordable computers that inspired a generation of tech enthusiasts.

But the real game-changer came on February 29, 2012, when the first Raspberry Pi was launched. This tiny titan, developed by the Raspberry Pi Foundation in the UK, was initially designed to promote basic computer science education in schools. Little did they know, they had uncorked a genie in a bottle! The Pi took the world by storm, revolutionizing not just education but every industry it touched. From humble beginnings to worldwide acclaim, SBCs have truly come a long way, my friend!

So, what's the secret sauce that makes these tiny computers so delectable? Well, they're powerful, affordable, and more than anything, they're versatile. Whether you're a farmer looking to monitor your crops or a gamer wanting to build your own console, SBCs like the Raspberry Pi are your ticket to ride. They're truly a testament to the saying, "great things come in small packages."

3.

Gary Covella, Ph.D.

Up next, we'll explore the nitty-gritty of how these petite powerhouses work, and how you can harness their potential to generate profits. Stay tuned, the journey is just getting started!

Hardware and Software Specifications

Let's dive headfirst into the meat and potatoes of our subject: the hardware and software specifications of these mighty minuscule machines. Like David facing Goliath, these small computers pack a wallop that belies their diminutive stature.

The Raspberry Pi, for instance, boasts a powerful ARM-based processor, a GPU, RAM, and multiple input/output (I/O) interfaces, all neatly tucked into a board no larger than your credit card. The latest version even includes Wi-Fi, Bluetooth, and Ethernet capabilities – talk about connectivity! It's like having an entire orchestra playing in harmony, all under the direction of one maestro.

Turning our attention to the software side, most SBCs, including the Raspberry Pi, run on Linux-based operating systems. This choice of software is no coincidence, my friend. Linux, being open-source, provides the flexibility and freedom for programmers to tinker, tweak, and tailor the system to their heart's content. Combine this with the power-packed hardware, and you've got a recipe for unlimited innovation!

So, whether you're an entrepreneur, an inventor, or an educator, these micro marvels are poised to transform your ideas into profitable endeavors. But hey, don't take my word for it! In the following chapters, we'll delve deeper into real-world applications and success stories that have leveraged the power of SBCs. Buckle up, because this ride is about to get even more exciting!

Importance of Open-Source Platforms

Open-source platforms, my dear reader, are the bread and butter of creative geniuses. A veritable treasure trove for tech enthusiasts, they are the playgrounds where ideas take flight and innovation kicks into overdrive. You see, the beauty of open-source lies not only in its accessibility but in its collaborative spirit. Developers from around the world can contribute, critique, and improve code, refining the platform and making it robust with the collective wisdom of a global community.

Now, why does it matter in the context of our heroic little computer? Simply put, when you pair the adaptability of open-source software with the power of a single-board computer like the Raspberry Pi, you're equipping yourself with a canvas primed for the birth of groundbreaking tech marvels. From coding your own video game to automating your entire home, the possibilities are as endless as your imagination.

But remember, open-source is more than just a tool; it's a philosophy. It's about tearing down walls and building bridges. It's about sharing knowledge freely and valuing community over competition. So, embrace it, contribute to it, and watch how it catapults your innovative ideas into the stratosphere of success.

Raspberry Pi Community and Its Significance

Oh, the Raspberry Pi community, my friend, is nothing short of a gold mine for innovators and inventors like you. Picture this: a bustling hub of bright minds tirelessly pushing the boundaries of what this tiny titan can do. It's a vibrant, inclusive, and collaborative ecosystem of enthusiasts who are just as passionate about the Raspberry Pi as you are.

You see, this community isn't just about tinkering with circuit boards and writing lines of code. It's about sharing triumphs, troubleshooting challenges, and sparking ideas that could very well change the world. From beginners seeking guidance to seasoned veterans sharing their cutting-edge projects, everyone adds value to this dynamic melting pot of innovation. Participating in this community, you're not just standing on the shoulders of giants – you're becoming one.

Dive headfirst into this pool of collective wisdom, share your queries, discuss your ideas, and watch as they evolve and flourish amidst this fertile ground of knowledge. Remember, the Raspberry Pi isn't just a computer; it's your ticket to a supportive community that will fuel your journey towards creating something extraordinary. So, become an active part of it, engage, learn, and grow. After all, the magic of the Raspberry Pi doesn't just lie in its hardware, but in the people who breathe life into it.

Different Models and Their Applications

The Raspberry Pi, this pocket-sized powerhouse, comes in a variety of models, each with its unique strengths and tailored to diverse applications.

For instance, the Raspberry Pi Zero, a lean mean machine, is perfect for low-cost and low-power projects. You see, this model is ideal for DIY solutions like wearables or weather stations where size and power consumption are critical.

Next in line, we have the Raspberry Pi 3 and 4 models. These are full-fledged mini-computers that can handle demanding tasks, like serving as a media center or even a desktop replacement. They're also perfect for IoT and home automation projects due to their onboard WiFi and Bluetooth capabilities.

And let's not forget the Raspberry Pi Pico, the newest member of the family.

Pi Profits

This microcontroller board is a godsend for hardware enthusiasts interested in embedded systems. Whether you're building a robot, crafting a digital thermometer, or dabbling in drone tech, the Pico has got you covered.

Each Raspberry Pi model serves as a versatile tool, capable of transforming your creative concepts into a tangible reality. But remember, choosing the right model for your project is crucial. Consider your project's requirements, budget, and complexity. Then, select the model that fits your needs like a glove because, my friend, a well-chosen Raspberry Pi is like a magic wand — it brings your imagination to life!

Accessories and Expansion Boards

Now that we've covered the different Raspberry Pi models, let's delve into the exciting world of accessories and expansion boards. These additions can amplify the capabilities of your chosen model, allowing you to push the boundaries of what's possible.

We're talking about camera modules for creating a DIY surveillance system or robotics project. Or how about an LCD touchscreen for designing your custom tablet or smart home controller? And we can't forget the expansive selection of HATs (Hardware Attached on Top). These expansion boards, specifically designed for Raspberry Pi, allow for functionalities like motor control, GPS, and even cellular communication.

But don't let the array of options overwhelm you. Like choosing your Raspberry Pi model, selecting the right accessories is all about aligning with your project's needs. Consider what you want your project to do, the space constraints you have to work with, and of course, your budget. With a well-thought-out selection of accessories, you can supercharge your Raspberry Pi and bring your most ambitious projects to life.

Remember, the world of Raspberry Pi is a treasure trove of innovation just waiting to be discovered. So, go ahead, pick your model, select your accessories, and let your imagination run wild. Trust me, there's no better time to start than now, and no better tool than Raspberry Pi.

Getting Started: Initial Setup

Setting up your Raspberry Pi for the first time might seem like a daunting task, but I assure you, it's easier than you'd imagine. All you need is your Raspberry Pi, a microSD card (at least 8GB), an HDMI monitor, a USB keyboard, and a power source. Now, let's dive in. First, you'll need to download the latest version of Raspberry Pi OS (formerly Raspbian) from the official Raspberry Pi website. Next, write the downloaded image to your microSD card using imaging software such as balenaEtcher. Once the image writing is complete, insert the microSD card into your Raspberry Pi, connect the monitor and keyboard, and finally, connect the power. Voila! Your Raspberry Pi will boot up, and you'll see a welcome screen. Follow the on-screen instructions to complete the setup. Remember, the beauty of Raspberry Pi lies in exploration and experimentation. It's like your personal playground for technological innovation — so don't be afraid to make mistakes and learn.

Gary Covella, Ph.D.

Raspberry Pi: Step-by-Step Set Up Guide

Prepare Your Tools: Gather your Raspberry Pi, a microSD card (with a minimum capacity of 8GB), an HDMI monitor, a USB keyboard, and a power source.

Download the Raspberry Pi OS: Visit the official Raspberry Pi website and download the latest version of Raspberry Pi OS (previously known as Raspbian).

Image Your microSD Card: Write the downloaded image to your microSD card using imaging software. balenaEtcher is a recommended option for this process.

Assemble Your Raspberry Pi: Once the image writing is complete, insert the microSD card into your Raspberry Pi. Next, connect the HDMI monitor and the USB keyboard.

Power Up: Finally, connect the power. Your Raspberry Pi will boot up and display a welcome screen.

Follow On-Screen Instructions: To complete the setup, simply follow the instructions displayed on the screen.

Pi Profits

Remember, the realm of Raspberry Pi is all about discovery and trial. Consider it your personal sandbox for technological innovation. Any mistakes you make will only bring more learning opportunities. So let your imagination run wild and get started!

Alright, now that you've got your Raspberry Pi up and running, it's time to dive into the ocean of information out there. And guess what? A lot of it is absolutely free! Here are a few websites that I personally find incredibly helpful:

Raspberry Pi Foundation - https://www.raspberrypi.org - These are the folks who made Raspberry Pi, and their website is a goldmine of tutorials, project ideas, and news on the latest developments.

GitHub - https://github.com/raspberrypi - This is where the Raspberry Pi Foundation and other enthusiasts share code. You'll find everything from simple scripts to full-blown project blueprints here.

Adafruit - https://learn.adafruit.com/category/raspberry-pi - Adafruit's Raspberry Pi section is chock-full of tutorials that are detailed, beginner-friendly, and cover a wide range of applications.

Pi My Life Up - https://pimylifeup.com/category/projects/raspberry-pi/ - This site boasts a massive collection of Raspberry Pi project guides. Their tutorials are easy to follow and cover a wide range of complexity levels, from beginner to advanced.

MagPi Magazine - https://magpi.raspberrypi.org - This is the official Raspberry Pi magazine. It's loaded with tutorials, reviews, and features about the Pi community. The best part? You can download every issue for free!

Remember, the Internet is a treasure trove of information. With a keen eye, a little patience, and a thirst for knowledge, you'll be amazed at what you can find.

Raspberry Pi OS Options and Installations

When it comes to choosing the optimal operating system for your Raspberry Pi, you've got quite a few tantalizing options. The official OS, Raspberry Pi OS (formerly known as Raspbian), is a solid choice for beginners. It's user-friendly, and it's decked out with everything you need to kickstart your projects. But don't let the "official" tag limit your choices. There's a whole world of alternatives out there.

For instance, if you're planning on turning your Pi into a retro gaming console, consider RetroPie. It's a specialized OS that transforms your Raspberry Pi into a gaming machine packed with pre-installed emulators for tons of gaming platforms.

Ubuntu and Windows IoT Core are also worth checking out. The former is a well-loved, versatile Linux distro, and the latter opens the doors to a vast array of Microsoft's development tools.

But remember, before you get started, you'll need to install your chosen OS on a microSD card. This process is straightforward and well-documented, especially for Raspberry Pi OS. Other OS may vary slightly, but don't fret — the Raspberry Pi community is always ready to lend a helping hand.

Gary Covella, Ph.D.

So, go ahead, choose an OS, roll up your sleeves, and let's dive right in. This tiny beast is waiting to unleash its power!

Alright, let's get your hands dirty with some Raspberry Pi OS websites and their corresponding URLs. Here's a list of some of the most popular ones:

Raspberry Pi OS – This is the official Raspberry Pi OS. Navigate through this website to get introduced to this user-friendly interface.

Ubuntu for Raspberry Pi – One of the most popular Linux distributions, Ubuntu offers a robust platform for your Raspberry Pi projects.

RetroPie – If you're a gaming enthusiast, this specialized OS is your jackpot. It's loaded with pre-installed emulators and turns your Raspberry Pi into a retro gaming console.

Windows 10 IoT Core – This OS is for those who prefer to work with Microsoft's development tools. It opens a wide array of opportunities for your Raspberry Pi device.

Remember, each of these websites is a treasure trove of information and resources. So don't just skim through them. Immerse yourself, explore, and learn. Your Raspberry Pi adventure is just getting started!

Potential Challenges and Troubleshooting Tips

Listen, we're not going to sugarcoat it for you. This isn't a walk in the park. There will be hurdles to jump over and pitfalls to avoid. But don't sweat it, that's where the real learning happens. So, let's talk about some of the potential challenges you might face with your Raspberry Pi.

First, you might encounter SD card issues, a common headache for Raspberry Pi users. The golden rule here is to ensure your SD card is properly formatted and has enough space.

Second, power supply problems. Your Raspberry Pi isn't your average device. It demands a power supply with at least 5V and 1.2A. Anything less and your Pi might not work as efficiently as it should.

Third, overheating. This tiny powerhouse can get hot under the collar when you're putting it to work. Consider investing in a heatsink or a fan to keep it cool.

But hey, don't be disheartened by these challenges. With every problem you encounter, you'll learn something new and become a more seasoned Raspberry Pi user. And remember, the Raspberry Pi community is always there to back you up. So, buckle up, embrace the challenges, and let's carve your success story with Raspberry Pi.

Raspberry Pi's Role in Democratizing Technology

The Raspberry Pi, this micro powerhouse, is more than just a trendy gadget for tech enthusiasts. It's an enabler, a democratizer of technology. Picture this, a computer that fits in the palm of your hand, costing less than a night out, yet holding the power to drive innovation across sectors. That's Raspberry Pi for you. What started as an educational tool is now at the heart of numerous technological advancements, levelling the playing field for innovators worldwide. Whether it's robotics, IoT, or digital art installations, the Raspberry Pi has proven its mettle. It's empowering tinkerers, hobbyists, and professionals alike, breaking down barriers to entry and making it easier for anyone with a vision to bring their ideas to life. The Raspberry Pi is not just a device; it's a revolution, a testimony that in the realm of technology, size doesn't determine power!

Harnessing the Potential of Raspberry Pi

So, how can you tap into this tiny yet potent computer's potential? The possibilities are endless! From automating your home to creating a retro gaming console, here are some exciting ventures that you can explore with Raspberry Pi:

Home Automation: With the help of sensors and actuators, you can turn your humble abode into a smart home using Raspberry Pi. Control your lights, temperature, and appliances from anywhere in the world with just a few lines of code.

Educational Tools: The Raspberry Pi is an excellent tool for educators to introduce students to coding, robotics, and other tech-related concepts. It's affordable and versatile, making it the perfect choice for schools and universities on a budget.

Digital Art Installations: Artists and creatives can use Raspberry Pi to bring their visions to life by creating interactive digital art installations. With its low cost and small size, it's an excellent alternative to traditional computing devices for multimedia projects.

Agricultural Tech: The Raspberry Pi can be used in agriculture to automate tasks such as irrigation systems, monitoring soil conditions, and managing livestock. Its low power consumption makes it ideal for off-grid applications.

Gaming Consoles: Want to relive the nostalgia of old-school gaming? With Raspberry Pi, you can build your own retro game console and play classic games from consoles like NES, SNES, and Sega Genesis.

Think Outside the Box

But don't limit yourself to just these ideas. The potential of Raspberry Pi

Pi Profits

extends far beyond these examples. With its affordability, versatility, and compact size, you can use it in almost any industry or field. Whether you're a tech enthusiast, entrepreneur, educator, or artist, this tiny computer has something to offer for everyone.

So go ahead and explore the endless possibilities with Raspberry Pi.

Gary Covella, Ph.D.

CHAPTER 2: BUILDING HOME AUTOMATION SYSTEMS

As we delve deeper into the era of smart technology, the concept of home automation has moved from the realm of science fiction to everyday reality. In this chapter, we'll explore how you can use the Raspberry Pi to design and implement a home automation system that can control a range of household devices. Imagine a home where your devices interact with each other, your lights adjust to your schedule, and your heating system knows when to crank up the temperature. Sounds intriguing, right? We're about to turn your home into a smart ecosystem, enhancing not only its efficiency but also your comfort and convenience.

Monetizing Raspberry Pi Powered Home Automation Systems

Eager to transform your Raspberry Pi tinkering into a money-making venture? You're in for a treat! In this burgeoning era of smart homes, your DIY Raspberry Pi home automation systems can be a goldmine. Let's explore how:

Customization and Installations: Every household has unique needs. Offering customized home automation solutions tailored to individual clients' requirements, preferences, and budgets can unlock a direct source of income. You can even provide installation services, ensuring the system's seamless integration into their home setup.

Maintenance and Upgrades: Automation systems require regular maintenance and periodic upgrades to remain efficient and up-to-date. Offering these services on a contract basis can ensure a consistent revenue stream.

Training and Consultation: Not everyone is tech-savvy. Providing training services to users on how to operate the system or offering consultation for potential smart home enthusiasts can be another lucrative outlet.

Remember, the key lies in understanding your client's needs, delivering exceptional service, and fostering trust. So, gear up and turn your

Raspberry Pi expertise into a thriving business!

Understanding the Demand for Home Automation

The allure of home automation is undeniable in the digital age. As technology continues to evolve, so does our pursuit for convenience and efficiency. More and more homeowners are seeking ways to make their homes "smarter". For instance, they want lights that turn off automatically when they leave the room, or thermostats that adjust the temperature based on their daily routines. This growing demand is fueled by the desire for increased comfort, energy efficiency, security, and the sheer convenience of controlling home appliances remotely. Additionally, the trend of 'aging in place' where seniors prefer to stay in their own homes rather than moving to retirement homes, has also contributed to this demand as home automation systems can provide them with increased safety and independence. Understanding these driving factors can help you position your Raspberry Pi home automation services to meet the needs of your potential clients effectively.

Gary Covella, Ph.D.

Basics of Sensors and Actuators

Sensors and actuators form the backbone of any home automation system, bridging the gap between the digital and physical world. Their role? To transform the Raspberry Pi into a conduit for real-world interaction.

The Role of Sensors in Home Automation

Sensors serve as the eyes and ears of your home automation system. They are the devices that detect changes in the environment. Whether it's a change in temperature, the detection of motion, or even the level of sunlight, sensors relay this information back to the Raspberry Pi. Common types of sensors used in home automation include temperature sensors, motion sensors, and light sensors. For instance, a light sensor can detect when it starts to get dark outside and signal the Raspberry Pi to turn on the lights in your home.

Actuators: The Movers and Shakers

If sensors are the eyes and ears, then actuators are the hands and legs of your home automation system. They perform actions based on the information received from the sensors and the instructions from the Raspberry Pi. This might include turning on a light, adjusting a thermostat, or even activating a security system. Common types of actuators include switches, motors, and valves.

Integrating Sensors and Actuators with Raspberry Pi

To get the most out of your Raspberry Pi home automation system, understanding how to appropriately integrate sensors and actuators is crucial. The Raspberry Pi interfaces with these components using its General Purpose Input/Output (GPIO) pins. These pins can be programmed to either send signals (actuator control) or receive signals (sensor feedback), allowing for dynamic interaction with the physical environment.

The possibilities with a Raspberry Pi, coupled with the right sensors and actuators, are truly staggering. From a plant watering system that responds to soil moisture levels, to a security system that can recognize familiar faces, the potential to innovate and customize is limited only by your imagination. So, get tinkering, testing, and transforming your abode into a smart home that not only works for you but also works with you.

Raspberry Pi GPIO: An Overview

The Raspberry Pi's General Purpose Input/Output (GPIO) pins are the secret sauce to its saucey versatility. These pins, neatly arrayed along the edge of the board, are the reason why this tiny computer can interact with the real world. With these pins, the Raspberry Pi can pick up inputs from sensors, flick on LEDs, trigger relays, or send signals to other devices. They are what allows a Raspberry Pi to automate a home, control a robot, or even run a makeshift gaming console. There's a world of opportunity in each pin – a world that this chapter will help you to explore.

But beware, my tech-savvy friends, these pins aren't just any old pins. They're a sort of chameleon; they can take on the role of input or output depending on your needs. You can use them to pick up data, or to send out orders. It's like having a personal army of Swiss army knives, each waiting for your command to morph into the tool you need. But to use this army, you need to understand it. So, buckle up, because we're about to take a deep dive into the world of Raspberry Pi GPIO. We'll cover everything from the basics of GPIO, to how to use it in your projects, and the endless possibilities that await. Are you ready? Let's go!

The Basics of Raspberry Pi GPIO

GPIO stands for General Purpose Input/Output, which is exactly what these pins do – they allow input and output from external devices. These pins can be configured as either inputs or outputs, depending on the needs of your project. Each pin can be individually programmed and controlled, giving you a high level of flexibility in your projects.

There are 40 GPIO pins on a Raspberry Pi, numbered from 0 to 39. These pins are divided into two main groups – the GPIO header and the P5 header. The GPIO header has 26 pins, while the P5 header has 14 pins. Each pin has a specific purpose and can be used for different tasks, making the Raspberry Pi a versatile tool for any project.

Input and Output

As mentioned before, GPIO pins can be configured as either input or output. An input pin allows the Raspberry Pi to receive data from external sensors or devices. This data can be in the form of digital signals, analog signals, or even serial communication.

On the other hand, an output pin allows the Raspberry Pi to send signals out to external devices. These signals can control LEDs, motors, relays, and more. By sending specific voltage levels, you can make these devices perform a variety of actions.

Designing Control Interfaces

The magic truly begins when you start to design control interfaces for your Raspberry Pi. Think of it as the bridge between your creative mind and the physical world. When you design a control interface, you're essentially defining how the Raspberry Pi interacts with external devices, be it a simple LED light or a complex robotic arm.

There are unlimited ways to design control interfaces, and the choice largely depends on the nature of your project. If you're building a cool, LED-lit gaming console, you might want to control the color and pattern of lights through GPIO. Or if you're automating your home, you can design an interface to control everything from temperature to music to lights with a few taps on your smartphone.

The key is to understand the capabilities of GPIO and how to leverage them effectively. Start by outlining your project, define the tasks that need to be automated or controlled, and then brainstorm the best ways to achieve this using the Raspberry Pi's GPIO pins.

Protocols: Zigbee, MQTT, and More

Now, let's dive into the heart of communication protocols. The Raspberry Pi supports a plethora of protocols, but we're going to focus on a couple of the big guns: Zigbee and MQTT.

Zigbee, often used in home automation systems, is a high-level communication protocol that creates networks — mesh networks to be specific. It's like a web of interconnected devices, where each node (device) is capable of communicating with its neighbors. This makes Zigbee robust and reliable, as the network can function even if a few nodes fail.

On the other hand, MQTT – standing for Message Queuing Telemetry Transport – is a publish-subscribe-based messaging protocol. It works like a post office. Your Raspberry Pi, acting as a publisher, sends messages to a MQTT broker (the post office), and any device that has subscribed to that broker (the recipients) receive the message. It's lightweight, simple, and perfect for IoT devices with limited processing capabilities.

Both Zigbee and MQTT have their strengths and ideal use-cases. If you're building a sensor network with multiple nodes, Zigbee could be your best bet. For simple, one-way communication between a Raspberry Pi and a few devices, MQTT might be more suitable. Ultimately, the protocol you choose will depend on the requirements of your project. Explore each protocol, understand their strengths and weaknesses, and make an informed decision. This is crucial in the grand scheme of your Raspberry Pi project.

Case Study: Smart Lighting System

Let's delve deeper into our case study – a Smart Lighting System. Imagine this: you walk into a room, and the lights automatically adjust to your preferred brightness and color temperature, setting the mood just right. This isn't some futuristic utopia; it's a reality made possible with Raspberry Pi and the right communication protocol.

In this scenario, a Raspberry Pi, acting as the central hub, interfaces with an array of smart light bulbs via Zigbee. Why Zigbee, you ask? Remember, Zigbee excels in creating mesh networks, perfect for systems containing multiple nodes that need to communicate with each other. In our smart lighting system, each light bulb acts as a node in the Zigbee network, receiving instructions from the Raspberry Pi and reporting its status back.

However, we also want our system to be remotely controllable, which is where

Gary Covella, Ph.D.

MQTT comes in. We can use MQTT to send commands from a smartphone app to the Raspberry Pi. Since MQTT is lightweight, it's perfect for this kind of simple, one-way communication.

With the right hardware and a bit of code, you could automate your entire home lighting system, creating an environment that responds to your needs without you lifting a finger. The possibilities are endless, and it's all at your fingertips with the power of Raspberry Pi. Remember, the key is understanding your project's requirements and choosing the right protocol. Explore, experiment, and let your creativity shine!

Case Study: Security Camera Integration

Let's take this a notch higher and consider another use case, the integration of a security camera system. Picture a world where you not only control your lights but also your home's security system, all from your smartphone. Now, with Raspberry Pi, this isn't a pipe dream anymore, it's a reality!

Pi Profits

Consider a setup where the Raspberry Pi acts as the central hub that interfaces with a variety of security cameras installed around your home. The cameras, acting as nodes in this network, stream live video feeds to the Raspberry Pi, which then processes the video and performs any desired actions, like detecting motion or recognizing faces.

We can again leverage MQTT for real-time alerts. If an anomaly is detected, the Raspberry Pi can send an MQTT message to your smartphone, notifying you instantly of the situation. Add to this the power of a video streaming protocol like RTSP, and you have a full-fledged security system capable of streaming live video to your device wherever you are.

With a pinch of creativity and some basic hardware, a Raspberry Pi can transform your home into a smart, secure fortress. The power to innovate and optimize is literally in your hands. Dive in, play around, and let your entrepreneurial spirit take flight!

Gary Covella, Ph.D.

Case Study: Smart Agricultural System

Shifting gears, let's journey into another groundbreaking use of the Raspberry Pi: smart agricultural systems. Yes, you read right! This diminutive device is also transforming the way we farm and grow our food. Picture a sustainable farm powered by technology, where every plant gets the exact amount of sunlight, water, and nutrients it needs. Sounds like science fiction? Well, with Raspberry Pi, it's science fact!

Imagine using your Raspberry Pi to monitor soil moisture levels in real-time, or to control irrigation systems based on weather forecasts. Or, how about a system that identifies pests on your plants and alerts you instantly? The possibilities are boundless and limited only by your imagination.

To set up such a system, you would need a Raspberry Pi, some sensors (for measuring things like soil moisture, temperature, and light), and actuators (to control things like water valves or light sources). MQTT could again serve as the communication protocol, allowing for real-time data collection and immediate actions.

Through smart agriculture, Raspberry Pi is helping farmers increase their yields, reduce waste, and improve sustainability. So, whether you're an urban gardener or a rural farmer, your Raspberry Pi could be the secret weapon for a more productive and sustainable future. Once again, the power to innovate rests in your hands. So why wait? Give it a shot and let the Raspberry Pi revolutionize your farming experience!

Voice-Controlled Automation with Raspberry Pi

You'd think that we've covered enough ground with our tiny friend, the Raspberry Pi, right? Well, hold onto your hats because this ride is far from over. Next up, we're diving into the world of voice-controlled automation with the Raspberry Pi. This isn't just fancy Star Trek talk, it's the real deal, and it's happening right now.

You see, the Raspberry Pi's prowess doesn't stop at smart agriculture systems. No, no, no, it's much more versatile than that. It can also be used to create a state-of-the-art voice-controlled automation system. Think Amazon's Alexa or Google's Assistant but personalized just for you. Want to turn on your living room lights with a simple command? Or maybe play your favorite tune when you walk in the door? Or how about brewing a fresh pot of coffee first thing in the morning, all without lifting a finger? All this and more is possible with the mighty Raspberry Pi.

You'll need a microphone and speaker, along with your Raspberry Pi for this project. We'll use a software like Mycroft or Alexa Skills Kit for the voice recognition and processing. And just like that, voila! You are the master commander of your abode. The Raspberry Pi, ever faithful, listens and obeys, bringing your wish to life.

This is not just something to boast about; it's a real game-changer. It's giving people with disabilities new levels of independence. It's providing comfort and convenience for everyone. And it's yet another way that Raspberry Pi is breaking boundaries and democratizing technology. So buckle up, folks! We're about to take voice control to a whole new level with Raspberry Pi.

Maintenance, Updates, and Troubleshooting

So, you've set up your voice-controlled Raspberry Pi system. It's the dawn of a new era in your household. Commands float through the air and tasks get done, all with the smooth efficiency of a spy movie. But hey, even top-notch tech needs a little TLC now and again. That's where maintenance, updates, and troubleshooting come in.

Just like a car needs oil changes, your voice-controlled Raspberry Pi system needs regular software updates. These updates come with new features, bug fixes, and security enhancements to keep your system running smoothly. You'll get them through the software you've chosen for voice recognition, whether it's Mycroft or Alexa Skills Kit.

But what about when things go awry? Maybe your Raspberry Pi isn't responding or it's acting a bit quirky. Don't sweat it, we've got you covered. The beauty of Raspberry Pi is its massive community of users. Online forums, tutorials, and guides abound. You'll find answers to common problems, advice for complicated issues, and tips to fine-tune your system.

Remember, maintenance and troubleshooting are just part of the gig when you're pushing the boundaries of what's possible. See them as opportunities to learn, grow, and perfect your voice-controlled automation system. It's all part of the journey in the remarkable world of Raspberry Pi.

Remotely Updating Your Raspberry Pi

Alright, let's dive into the nitty-gritty. You've got your Raspberry Pi humming along nicely and now you want to remotely update it, right? Well, sit back, relax, and let's ride this digital wave together.

The first thing you want to do is set up a secure shell (SSH) on your Raspberry Pi. SSH is like a private chat room for your computer and Raspberry Pi. It's secure, encrypted, and perfect for remote connections. So, no matter where you are in the world, you can chat with your Raspberry Pi and give it the latest software updates.

You can enable SSH using the Raspberry Pi configuration settings. Once that's done, you'll need the Pi's IP address. Enter this into your SSH client — if you're on Windows, you can use PuTTY; Mac and Linux users can just use the terminal. Punch in your Pi's credentials and voila, you're in!

Now, updating is as easy as inputting a couple of commands: `sudo apt update` followed by `sudo apt upgrade`. The first command tells your Pi to fetch the latest updates, and the second applies them. Pat yourself on the back, you've just remotely updated your Raspberry Pi!

Remember, with great power comes great responsibility — or in this case, with remote access comes the need for strong security. Make sure you change your Raspberry Pi's default password to something a little more cryptic.

Alright, let's say you're not just a tech enthusiast, but you've got yourself a fully-fledged home automation business. You're helping people transform their humble abodes into futuristic smart homes using the power of Raspberry Pi. So how does remote updating fit into this?

Well, imagine this scenario — you've got a customer, let's call him Bob. You helped Bob automate his home six months ago. But technology moves fast, and there's new software that could make Bob's system even better. But Bob isn't tech-savvy. He wouldn't know his SSH from his elbow. So, what do you do? You take advantage of remote updating.

With the SSH we've just set up, you can log into Bob's Raspberry Pi from your own office. You can update his system with the latest and greatest software, making sure his home is as smart as can be. All without making a house call. And let's face it, in today's fast-paced world, convenience is king.

Here's the kicker. Not only does this service make life easier for your customers, it also adds another income stream for your business. You could offer this as a regular maintenance package — let's call it 'Pi Care'. For a small monthly fee, you ensure their systems are always up-to-date, secure, and running smoothly.

Now that's what I call working smarter, not harder. It's a win-win situation, and it's all thanks to the power of Raspberry Pi and remote updating. So, go ahead, power up your home automation business with this nifty trick up your sleeve.

Pricing and Selling Home Automation Solutions

Sure, you're stepping up your game with the Raspberry Pi, offering top-notch home automation solutions and providing outstanding customer service with remote updates. But the pivotal question remains — how do you price and sell these innovative solutions?

Pricing is a critical factor that could make or break your business. The trick is in striking a sweet balance — you don't want to undersell your services, nor do you want to price yourself out of the market. Do some market research. Understand what your competitors are offering and at what price. You've got an added advantage with your unique 'Pi Care' maintenance package — be sure to factor that into your pricing.

Gary Covella, Ph.D.

Once you've got your pricing figured
out, it's time to sell. And remember,
you're not just selling a product or
service - you're selling a solution, an
experience, a lifestyle. You're selling
the ease and convenience of a smart home
that's always up-to-date, always secure,
always performing at its best. You're
selling the peace of mind that comes
with knowing there's a tech expert just
an SSH away.

Marketing plays a key role here. Start
with the traditional channels - your
website, emails, social media. But don't
stop there. Explore newer avenues to
reach your target audience. How about
webinars or workshops showing people the
benefits of home automation? Or
collaborations with local tech stores or
home improvement shops?

Remember, every home is a potential
customer. Every homeowner who values
convenience, security, and cutting-edge
technology is a potential customer.
Reach out to them, show them the power
of Raspberry Pi, and watch your business
soar.

And finally, don't forget the power of
testimonials. There's no better
marketing strategy than a satisfied

44.

customer. Encourage your happy customers to spread the word. Offer incentives for referrals. After all, word-of-mouth is a powerful tool in the arsenal of a successful business.

So there you have it, folks. Pricing and selling your home automation solutions might seem like a daunting task, but with some research, a bit of creativity, and a whole lot of passion for what you do, you'll be on your way to entrepreneurial success. And remember, when it comes to home automation with Raspberry Pi, the sky's the limit.

Well, let's get down to brass tacks and talk about pricing. For instance, for a simple Raspberry Pi model B, you might look at charging around $35. But remember, you aren't just selling a gadget, you're selling a solution. Now, if you've integrated this little powerhouse into a home automation kit, the value goes up. For a basic home security package, including a Raspberry Pi, camera module, motion sensor, and the necessary software, you might charge around $120 to $150.

Let's kick things up a notch and talk about a complete smart home package. This could include security, lighting,

climate control, and even entertainment
systems, all controlled from a central
hub powered by Raspberry Pi and tailored
to the customer's needs. For this, you
might charge anywhere from $500 to
$1000, or even more, depending on the
complexity and customization involved.

Remember, you're offering an innovative
solution that saves time and enhances
the convenience and security of a home.
Your pricing should reflect the value
you provide, not just the cost of the
components. Now, go out there and show
them what you've got!

Pi Profits

Gary Covella, Ph.D.

CHAPTER 3: CRAFTING A RETRO GAMING CONSOLE

Alright, you've automated homes and made life a breeze for some happy folks out there. Time to shift gears and cater to the gamers. Yes, you heard it right. We're about to step into the realm of retro gaming, creating a console with our mighty Raspberry Pi. So buckle up, because we're taking a trip down memory lane where pixels rule and sound chips create symphonies. We're going to turn nostalgia into lucrative business. My friends, welcome to Chapter 3: Crafting a Retro Gaming Console.

Why Retro Gaming?

The gaming industry is constantly evolving, with new consoles and games being released every year. But amidst all the glitz and glamour of modern gaming, there's still a demand for the classics. Whether it's to relive childhood memories or simply experience vintage gameplay, retro gaming has its dedicated fan base.

49.

Gary Covella, Ph.D.

By tapping into this market, you can cater to a niche audience and potentially generate significant revenue. Not to mention, creating a retro gaming console using Raspberry Pi allows for endless customization, making it a unique product in the market.

Materials Needed

Raspberry Pi (preferably model 3 or higher)

MicroSD card (minimum 8GB)

HDMI cable

Power supply

USB game controller(s)

RetroPie software (free to download)

TV or monitor

Step-by-Step Guide

Step 1: Download and Install RetroPie

First things first, we need the operating system that will allow us to emulate retro games. Head over to the RetroPie website and download the latest version of their software.

Pi Profits

Once downloaded, follow the instructions to install RetroPie on your Raspberry Pi.

Step 2: Insert MicroSD Card

Insert the microSD card into your Raspberry Pi. This is where the operating system and games will be stored.

Step 3: Connect Raspberry Pi to TV or Monitor

Use an HDMI cable to connect your Raspberry Pi to a TV or monitor. Make sure the input source on your TV or monitor is set to the correct HDMI port.

Step 4: Connect Game Controller(s)

Connect your USB game controller(s) to the Raspberry Pi. If you're using a wireless controller, you may need an adapter or Bluetooth connectivity.

Step 5: Power Up

Plug in the power supply to turn on your Raspberry Pi and RetroPie.

Gary Covella, Ph.D.

Step 6: Configure RetroPie

Once RetroPie is loaded, you'll be prompted to configure your game controller. Follow the instructions on the screen to map out the buttons on your controller.

Step 7: Add Games

Now it's time to add some games! You can do this in two ways:

Transfer ROMs from a USB drive to the "roms" folder on your Raspberry Pi.

Connect to your Wi-Fi network and transfer ROMs wirelessly using FileZilla or a similar program.

Step 8: Organize Games

To make it easier to find your games, create folders for different systems (e.g. NES, SNES, Sega Genesis) within the "roms" folder. You can also add custom box art and descriptions for each game by placing them in the "metadata" folder.

Step 9: Time to Play!

With RetroPie configured and games added, it's time to relive your favorite childhood memories! Simply select a game from the menu and hit play.

But don't limit yourself to just playing retro games – the Raspberry Pi is a versatile tool that can be used for various projects and ventures. From home automation to creating DIY arcade cabinets, the possibilities are endless.

So go ahead, explore and experiment with your Raspberry Pi to discover new and exciting opportunities. And who knows, you might just stumble upon the next big idea that could change the world! The only limit is your imagination.

Gaming Nostalgia and the Demand for Retro Gaming

The resurgence of retro gaming, driven by a wave of nostalgia, has created a booming market for vintage games. Amidst this resurgence, the Raspberry Pi emerges as a defining tool, enabling you to tap into the profitability of this trend. This versatile microcomputer not only allows you to relive your favorite

childhood games but also serves as a
gateway to countless innovative
projects. Whether you're interested in
home automation, creating DIY arcade
cabinets, or even exploring realms
beyond gaming, the Raspberry Pi provides
the platform you need. Harness its
potential to transform your innovative
ideas into lucrative ventures. As you
delve deeper into the world of Raspberry
Pi, remember, the only limit is your
imagination. Clouded by nostalgia,
powered by innovation — the future of
retro gaming lies within your grasp.

Emulation and RetroPie: A Match Made in Gaming Heaven

Emulation is a powerful technology that
recreates the hardware of old game
systems, allowing your Raspberry Pi to
run classic games. The process works by
imitating the behavior of one system
(say a vintage Sega console) on a
different system (the Raspberry Pi).
This is where RetroPie enters the scene.

RetroPie is a software library used to
emulate retro video games on the
Raspberry Pi computer. It's a
comprehensive, user-friendly tool that
brings your favorite vintage games back

to life. Picture this: the thrill of playing your cherished childhood games, now easily accessible on a single, compact, and cost-effective device.

Together, Emulation and RetroPie turn your Raspberry Pi into a retro gaming powerhouse. Whether you're looking to recreate an old gaming system, or to step into a growing market of retro enthusiasts, these tools provide you with the technology you need. And the best part? You don't have to be a tech guru to get started. So, roll up your sleeves and get ready to take a nostalgic trip down memory lane. Remember, with Raspberry Pi, your creativity is the only limit.

Game Sourcing and Copyright Considerations

When you're gearing up to relive your gaming glory days or introduce classic titles to a new generation of gamers, the question of where to source games from becomes paramount. There is a vast array of online platforms offering ROMs – the game files used by emulators – of vintage games. However, it's crucial to tread carefully, as not every ROM you stumble upon online is legal to use.

Gary Covella, Ph.D.

"But wait!" you might exclaim, "These are old games! Surely they're in the public domain by now?" Not so fast, my friend. This is where copyright considerations come into play. Just because a game was released decades ago doesn't mean it's free to download and use. Most classic games still retain their copyright protections, meaning unauthorized distribution and use of ROMs can land you in hot water. Therefore, it's essential to source your games responsibly, and always respect the rights of game developers and publishers.

In the world of Raspberry Pi and retro gaming, it's all fun and games until someone breaks the copyright laws. So, play it cool, play it safe, and above all, play it legal. Your nostalgic gaming journey begins here, but with the right moves, it doesn't have to end in a legal quagmire.

Controller Configurations and Options

Once you've legally sourced your games, the next step in your Raspberry Pi gaming odyssey is to configure your controllers. Now, this is where things get exciting! Raspberry Pi offers a myriad of controller options, each lending a different flavor to your gaming experience. From traditional gamepads to joystick controllers, the choice is truly yours.

If you're a stickler for authenticity, you might want to opt for a controller that matches the original console's design - for that extra dash of nostalgia. Or, if you fancy a modern twist, you could go for a wireless Bluetooth controller, offering the freedom to game from anywhere in your room.

Configuring your controller with Raspberry Pi is a breeze. The system automatically detects most USB controllers, and for Bluetooth controllers, it's as simple as pairing and selecting from a list. However, you'll want to pay attention to button mapping - ensuring that the controls correlate accurately with the on-screen actions.

Take your time to explore the options and find what feels best in your hands. The right controller can make the difference between a good gaming experience and an unforgettable one. So remember, in the realm of Raspberry Pi gaming, your controller is not just a tool, it's your weapon, your steering wheel, your magic wand. Choose it wisely and use it well!

Customizing the User Interface

Your Raspberry Pi gaming journey doesn't stop at controllers. Another joy of this little wonder-machine is the sheer level of customization it offers for the User Interface (UI). The beauty of the UI lies in its flexibility. You can tweak it, refine it, and even overhaul it to reflect your gaming persona.

With Raspberry Pi, the UI becomes a canvas for your creativity. From retro DOS-like interfaces to sleek, modern layouts, the possibilities are nearly endless. If you're a fan of the good old days, you might prefer a pixelated, 8-bit style layout that takes you back down memory lane. Or perhaps you fancy a futuristic sci-fi theme, complete with neon accents and cool animations.

But the Raspberry Pi doesn't stop at aesthetics. You can also customize functionality to your heart's content.

You can sort games by genre, console, or your own custom categories. Even better, you can add game metadata, such as descriptions, box art, and even ratings.

In essence, Raspberry Pi invites you to make your gaming experience truly personal. To craft a space that not only plays like a dream but feels like one. So dive in, experiment, and remember: In the world of Raspberry Pi, your gaming world is limited only by your imagination.

Multiplayer Setups and Network Play

Beyond the realm of solo gaming, Raspberry Pi opens up a whole new dimension: Multiplayer setups and online gaming. This tiny powerhouse has the capability to connect gamers across the globe, erasing geographical boundaries and bringing people together in the shared joy of gaming.

Whether you want to relive the nostalgia of old school LAN parties or compete in modern-day MMORPGs, Raspberry Pi's got your back. With the right setup, you can host your own gaming servers, or connect to existing ones and join in the fun.

And the best part is, you aren't limited to just Raspberry Pi users. Play with friends whether they're on a Raspberry Pi or a high-end gaming PC.

For those of you who prefer local multiplayer, Raspberry Pi still shines. You can hook up multiple controllers, split the screen, and dive into a frenzied race or a strategic battle with your buddies right in your living room.

At the end of the day, Raspberry Pi is not just about playing games, it's about sharing experiences, making connections, fostering competition, and building communities. It's about creating unforgettable moments of triumph, laughter, and camaraderie. So gear up, gather your friends, and embark on an exciting adventure in the vast universe of multiplayer gaming with Raspberry Pi.

Adding Non-Gaming Media to RetroPie

Introducing RetroPie, your one-stop media center solution. This ain't just about gaming anymore, my friends. This micro wonder now invites you to transform your Raspberry Pi into a full-fledged entertainment unit. Music, movies, TV shows, you name it, RetroPie can handle it. Here's the crazy part, with minimal effort, you can add your favorite non-gaming media into the RetroPie setup.

Now you can flip between an intense gaming session to a relaxing movie or groove to your favorite tracks with just a few clicks. All you gotta do is configure the Kodi Media Center on your RetroPie. Once you've got this setup, the world is your oyster. You can stream media content straight from your local network or the internet.

But let's not forget, in the heart of it all, it's about creating moments, experiences that last a lifetime. So why limit those experiences to games alone? Expand your horizons, amp up your entertainment, and immerse yourself in the awe-inspiring universe of multimedia with Raspberry Pi and RetroPie.

Packaging and Branding the Console

Alright, let's dive into the next big thing - packaging and branding your Raspberry Pi console. Now, listen up, I ain't talking about wrapping it up in a fancy box and calling it a day. No, sir! This is about creating a brand, an identity for your creation. Remember, people don't just buy a product, they buy the story, the emotion behind it.

Here's the deal. Before you start selling your console, you've got to make it look like a million bucks. From choosing a sleek case to designing an attractive logo, every detail matters. Thoughtful branding sets you apart from the crowd and adds value to your product. It's like a signature dish; it's got to have your unique touch.

Consider customizing the interface, creating unique themes, or even adding personalized boot-up messages. These small touches can take your console from being just another gadget to a memorable piece of tech. And remember, this ain't just business, it's personal. So, put your creativity into gear and let's make your console a real game-changer!

Customer Support and Updates

After-sales, the Silent Hero of Your Venture

Pi Profits

Now, I don't need to tell you this, but I will anyway; the game doesn't end once a product is in the customer's hands. In fact, that's just the beginning. You've created an unforgettable product, built an appealing brand, but there's one piece of the puzzle left — customer support and updates.

Customer support ain't just about problem-solving, it's about showing your customers that you're there for them, come rain or shine. It's about empathy, patience, and a good ear to listen. And let me tell you, a good support team can make or break your venture, that's no lie.

Don't treat updates as a chore either, pal. Updates keep your console fresh, exciting, and ticking along like a well-oiled machine. A console that's frequently updated is like a surprise gift, keeping your customers hooked and eager for more.

Remember, in this game, stagnation is your enemy. Always strive for better, for more. Learn from your customers, tweak your product, and watch your venture thrive.

Remote Support: Your Digital Lifeline

Gary Covella, Ph.D.

Alright, let's face it, we're living in a digital era where the world is just a click away. You've gotta meet your customers where they are, and most times, that's online. So, how can you lend a hand when you're miles away? Simple answer, my friend, remote support.

Remote support is like having a magic wand; it lets you troubleshoot issues without even being in the same room as the console! You can diagnose, guide, and even control their device remotely to resolve issues. It saves time, boosts customer satisfaction, and paints you as a real tech wizard.

But remember, power comes with responsibility. Keep your customer's privacy in mind at all times. Ask for their permission before accessing their device and respect their boundaries. This isn't just about solving problems; it's about building trust. So, invest in good remote support tools, train your team well, and let your magic wand do its wonders.

Remember, you're not just providing support; you're building relationships. And with remote support, you get to do this on a global scale.

Pi Profits

Marketing and Sales Channels for Retro Consoles

Alright, you've developed your console, got a solid support team, and an innovative update plan. Now, it's time to talk business, the lifeblood of your venture - marketing and sales. And I'm not just talking about running ads or tossing your console onto an online marketplace, that's child's play. No, my friend, you need a strategy, a game plan.

First off, identify your target audience. Are they old-school gamers, nostalgic for the classics? Or are they tech enthusiasts, always on the hunt for the next best gadget? Once you've got your audience pinned down, it's time to choose your battlefield, your sales channels.

Now, there's no one-size-fits-all here; you've got to figure out where your audience lives. Online stores, tech conventions, social media, gaming forums, the options are limitless. Just remember, where your audience is, there you should be too.

No product ever sold itself, so you've got to shout about your console from the rooftops. Make your marketing as unique as your console. Be bold, be brave, be heard. Now, go forth and conquer!

All set to get your marketing gears grinding? Great! Let's kick things off with some good old-fashioned content marketing. Start a blog, publish articles about your console's unique features, the technology behind it, and the games it can play. Better yet, create some video content. Unboxing videos, gameplay demos, behind-the-scenes looks at your development process - these can really drum up excitement.

Next, consider influencer marketing. Reach out to popular gaming influencers and tech reviewers on platforms like YouTube, Twitch, and Instagram. Send them a console for review, or partner with them for giveaways. Their word can go a long way in boosting your console's credibility and visibility.

Don't forget about social media advertising. Targeted ads on platforms where your audience hangs out can be an effective way to reach potential customers. Showcase your console's unique selling points in your ads to make them stand out.

Pi Profits

Last, but certainly not least, email
marketing. It's an oldie, but a goldie.
Collect email addresses through your
website and start sending out
newsletters. Updates about your console,
upcoming games, special promotions —
these can keep your audience engaged and
turn potential buyers into loyal
customers.

Now, these are just a few ideas to get
you started. The world of marketing is
vast and full of opportunities, so don't
be afraid to try out new strategies.
Remember, the goal is to get your
console into the hands of gamers, and to
do that, you need to be where they are.
So go on, make some noise, and let the
world know about your awesome console!

Gary Covella, Ph.D.

CHAPTER 4: EDUCATION WORKSHOPS AND RASPBERRY PI

Welcome to Chapter 4: a journey into the powerful combination of education workshops and Raspberry Pi. This small computer has brought about a paradigm shift in the sphere of educational technology. It's not just an innovation, it's an inspiration, a tool that unlocks creativity and cultivates critical thinking skills. In this chapter, we will delve into how educators and students can use Raspberry Pi to transform traditional learning methods into interactive, engaging experiences. So, let's roll up our sleeves, brew some coffee, and navigate the fascinating world of Raspberry Pi in education!

The Value of Tech Education in Today's World

In our rapidly evolving digital world, tech education holds tremendous value. It equips learners with the skills required to navigate the complexities of a technology-driven society and the ever-changing job market. More than just learning about hardware and software, tech education nurtures problem-solving skills, logical thinking, and creativity.

Enter Raspberry Pi, a tiny and affordable computer that's revolutionizing the way tech education is delivered. With Raspberry Pi, students get hands-on experience in coding and hardware configuration, breaking away from the mundane chalk-and-talk pedagogy. It empowers students to explore, invent, and learn at their own pace, hence fostering a self-learning culture. Raspberry Pi also provides an avenue for project-based learning, where students can apply their acquired knowledge to create something meaningful and practical, such as a weather station, or a home automation system.

This practicality of Raspberry Pi is what makes it an excellent tool for tech education. It brings abstract concepts to life, making learning fun, interesting, and most importantly, effective. It builds a strong foundation for students, preparing them for a future where digital literacy will be as essential as the three R's - reading, 'riting, and 'rithmetic.

So, whether you're an educator looking to make your classes more engaging, or a student seeking to deepen your understanding of technology, Raspberry Pi is a game-changer. Dive in, explore its possibilities, and watch as it transforms your educational journey!

Curriculum Design Principles

Building a potent curriculum around Raspberry Pi is akin to preparing a well-seasoned, mouth-watering dish. You start with the right ingredients (the hardware and software), add a dash of creativity, a spoonful of problem-solving, and a generous pinch of practical applications. Voila! You have a recipe for a rewarding, future-oriented learning experience that keeps students hooked.

Your Raspberry Pi curriculum should be designed to gradually introduce students to the basic concepts before diving into more complex topics. Begin with the building blocks, such as setting up the Raspberry Pi, understanding the command line, and getting familiar with Python programming. From there, gradually increase the complexity of the projects, introducing students to advanced concepts like GPIO control, networking, and data handling.

Remember, the purpose isn't just to teach students how to code, but to help them understand how that code interacts with the real world. So, incorporate projects that allow students to apply their knowledge in real-world scenarios. Let them build a simple robot or a digital photo frame. Let them experience the thrill of seeing their code spring to life, manifesting in physical, tangible outcomes.

This blend of theory and practice, combined with the flexibility to learn at their own pace, creates an engaging and effective learning environment. Students aren't just learning about technology, they're understanding its impact, and most importantly, they're having fun doing it. So, get on board the Raspberry Pi express and give your students a ticket to a future filled with endless possibilities.

Hands-On Projects for Beginners

Let's kickstart this journey with a project that never fails to spark curiosity and wonder – home automation. Turn your humble abode into a smart home using the might and magic of Raspberry Pi. This beginner-friendly project is a fantastic way to get your hands dirty in the realm of IoT (Internet of Things).

Control your home's lighting, heating, and even security systems with a few lines of Python code. Set up your Raspberry Pi to turn lights on at sunset or to heat your home before you arrive from work. With a bit of tinkering, you can even create a security system that sends you an email alert when it detects motion!

This hands-on project not only introduces you to the fundamentals of automation but also underscores the transformative potential of Raspberry Pi. You'll see how this tiny computer can make a huge difference in everyday life, acting as a conduit for creativity, innovation, and problem-solving. So, roll up your sleeves and transform your house into a smart home with the power of Raspberry Pi.

Raspberry Pi Powered Retro Gaming Console

After you've experienced the wonders of home automation, why not take your Raspberry Pi skills a step further? Let's dive into the world of retro gaming. Revisit the golden era of arcade games by constructing your very own Raspberry Pi powered gaming console. This exciting project will not only enhance your programming skills, but also ignite a sense of nostalgia with classic games like Pac-Man, Donkey Kong, and Space Invaders.

Harnessing the power of emulators such as RetroPie, you can transform your Raspberry Pi into a gaming powerhouse, capable of running thousands of games from countless classic consoles. Create a custom controller using simple components available online, or even repurpose an old one gathering dust. You'll learn about GPIO pins, wiring, Python scripts, and user interface design, all while having a blast from the past.

Remember, the objective here isn't just to build a gaming console but to understand the endless possibilities this tiny computer holds. As you delve deeper, you'll discover that Raspberry Pi isn't just about fun and games. It's a gateway to a dynamic world where technology and creativity intersect. So, ready to power up your Raspberry Pi gaming console?

Software Programming with Python on Raspberry Pi

Understanding the ins and outs of Python – one of the most popular and versatile programming languages – is crucial to unlocking the true potential of Raspberry Pi. This open-source language is the beating heart of numerous Raspberry Pi projects, powering everything from games to weather stations. Python's simplicity and readability make it an excellent choice for beginners, yet its depth and power are enough to satisfy even the most seasoned programmers.

In this chapter, we'll delve into the fundamentals of Python programming on Raspberry Pi. We'll start by setting up your coding environment, then move on to writing your first Python script. As you progress, you'll gain hands-on experience with Python's syntax, data structures, control flow, and libraries. You'll also learn how to interface with the Raspberry Pi's GPIO pins using Python, allowing you to control and interact with the physical world.

By mastering Python, you're not just learning a programming language. You're opening the door to a world of creative and entrepreneurial possibilities. Dive in, and let's start scripting our future with Python and Raspberry Pi. So why wait any longer? Let's get started!

The Power of Python

As mentioned earlier, Python is a versatile language that can be used for a wide range of applications. Its robust libraries and user-friendly syntax make it an excellent choice for developing projects on Raspberry Pi.

One of the most significant advantages of using Python is its flexibility. Being an interpreted language, it doesn't require a lengthy compilation process. This makes it perfect for rapid prototyping and experimentation. Plus, Python's dynamic typing allows you to change variable types as needed, making it easy to adapt your code on the fly.

Moreover, Python is a high-level language with a strong focus on readability and simplicity. This makes it an ideal choice for beginners who are just starting their coding journey. And with its increasing popularity, there is a wealth of resources available for learning and mastering Python.

Setting up your environment

Before we dive into writing code, it's essential to set up our Raspberry Pi for Python programming. Don't worry; it's a straightforward process.

First, make sure you have the latest version of Raspbian installed on your Raspberry Pi. If not, you can download it from the Raspberry Pi website and follow the installation instructions.

Next, open a terminal window by clicking on the icon in the toolbar or pressing Ctrl+Alt+T on your keyboard. In the terminal, type in "sudo apt-get update" to ensure that all packages are up to date.

Once that's done, we can install Python by typing in "sudo apt-get install python3" and pressing enter. This will install the latest version of Python on your Raspberry Pi.

Now that we have our environment set up, we're ready to dive into the exciting world of Python programming on Raspberry Pi.

The possibilities are endless.

With our environment all set up, let's take a moment to appreciate the possibilities that Python brings to the table. As mentioned earlier, Python is versatile and can be used in a wide range of applications.

For starters, you can use Python to automate tasks on your Raspberry Pi. This could include anything from controlling your smart home devices to scheduling backups for your important files.

Python is also highly popular in data science and machine learning thanks to its powerful libraries and frameworks. With the right skills, you can use Python to analyze data and build predictive models.

Additionally, Python is a great language for creating games and interactive applications. Its simple syntax makes it easy to learn and implement even complex game mechanics.

And that's not all — Python can also be used in fields like agriculture, art, education, and more. The possibilities are endless and limited only by your imagination.

Get Inspired by Success Stories

If you're feeling unsure about how to apply Python on Raspberry Pi, a great way to get inspired is by learning from others who have already done it. There are countless success stories of people using Python on their Raspberry Pi for various purposes.

For example, one teacher in Ireland used Python and Raspberry Pi to create a smart gardening system for her students. This not only taught the students about coding and technology, but also helped them take care of their school's garden.

Another success story comes from a software engineer who used Python and

Raspberry Pi to build a home security system. With just a few lines of code, he was able to control his home's lights, cameras, and alarms remotely using his smartphone.

The possibilities are truly endless with Python on Raspberry Pi. So don't hesitate to explore and experiment with this powerful combination. Who knows, you may just come up with the next big idea that changes the world! So, go ahead and dive into the captivating world of Python on Raspberry Pi — the only limit is your imagination.

Organizing and Promoting Workshops

Taking the plunge into the world of Raspberry Pi and Python opens up a wealth of opportunities to share your knowledge and inspire others. One surefire way is by organizing and promoting workshops. These can be a great platform to introduce novices to this powerful technology duo, or to help seasoned tech enthusiasts refine their skills.

You can tailor your workshops to cover a range of topics, from the basics of setting up a Raspberry Pi and writing your first lines of Python code, to constructing intricate automated systems or innovative art installations. To promote your workshop, leverage social media platforms where tech enthusiasts gather. Consider posting on forums like GitHub or Stack Overflow. If you're aiming for a local audience, network at tech meetups or university clubs.

Remember, every workshop you run adds a ripple to the wave of tech innovation. So, don't just dwell on the sidelines. Get out there, share your skills, and help shape the future with Raspberry Pi and Python. And who knows, you may even find yourself collaborating on groundbreaking projects with like-minded individuals! The possibilities are truly endless, so go ahead and start organizing your first workshop today. Let's spread the word about this game-changing technology and inspire others to join the Raspberry Pi community.

So keep exploring, keep innovating, and keep promoting. Together, we can take Raspberry Pi and Python to new heights and make a tangible impact on the world around us. Remember, the only limit is your imagination! So take that leap of faith, and get started today. The possibilities are waiting for you.

Providing Remote Learning Options

With the rise of digital learning platforms, we can now bring the power of Raspberry Pi and Python right to the students' doorstep. Remote learning opens up a universe of possibilities, making technological education accessible to everyone, regardless of their location. By creating and offering online courses, you can reach out to a much wider audience. Tailor your lessons for different skill levels, from beginners to advanced users.

Interactivity is key when it comes to online learning. Incorporate engaging resources like videos, quizzes, and discussion forums to enhance the learning experience. Live webinars where students can ask questions and get immediate responses would also bring tremendous value to your courses.

Offering remote learning options not only democratizes tech education but also can provide a consistent income stream. As a bonus, you're helping to nurture the next generation of tech innovators. So, consider going digital with your tech workshops and join the revolution in education. Raspberry Pi and Python are waiting to spark minds across the globe, and you could be the one to ignite that spark!

Embracing the Maker Movement

The maker movement is a global community of individuals who love to create, tinker, and innovate. It's all about taking a hands-on approach to learning by building tangible projects. Raspberry Pi and Python are perfect tools for makers of all ages and skill levels. With its small size, low cost, and endless possibilities, Raspberry Pi has become a staple in the maker community. And with Python's user-friendly and versatile nature, it's the perfect programming language for bringing ideas to life on Raspberry Pi.

So, whether you're an educator looking to engage students in hands-on learning, or an artist wanting to incorporate technology into your creations, the maker movement welcomes you with open arms. With Raspberry Pi and Python, the

only limit is your imagination. Let's
join forces and embrace the maker
movement together.

Ensuring Safety and Inclusivity in Workshops

While we zealously plunge into the world
of making and innovating, it's paramount
that we don't overlook the importance of
safety and inclusivity. Workshops,
whether virtual or in-person, must be a
sanctuary where one can learn, explore,
and create fearlessly. Raspberry Pi and
Python workshops should be no exception.

It's crucial to ensure that appropriate
safety measures are in place, especially
in sessions where hardware manipulation
is involved. Simple steps like providing
protective equipment, maintaining a
clutter-free workspace, and giving clear
instructions can significantly decrease
the risk of accidents.

Furthermore, inclusivity should not be
an afterthought but an integral part of
planning and conducting workshops. This
involves making sure that workshops are
accessible to people from diverse
backgrounds, skill levels, and
abilities. It might be as

straightforward as ensuring that your workshop materials are easy to understand, or as intricate as providing closed captions for your online tutorials. Remember, a truly inclusive workshop is not just about accommodating everyone; it's about making everyone feel welcome and valued. Let's strive to create a safe and inclusive environment where everyone can enjoy the thrill of bringing their ideas to life with Raspberry Pi and Python.

Feedback Mechanisms and Continuous Improvement

Just as it is vital to maintain safety and inclusivity, constructive feedback and continuous improvement form the lifeblood of any successful workshop. Every participant is a treasure trove of insights waiting to be unlocked, and their perspective can provide invaluable information to enhance the quality of future workshops.

Consider developing a structured feedback mechanism that not only invites participants' thoughts on what worked well in the workshop, but also their suggestions for areas of improvement. This could be in the form of a simple

survey questionnaire given at the end of
the session, or a more interactive
discussion.

The key here is to be receptive to the
input received and be ready to iterate
your workshop model based on the
feedback. Also, it's just as important
to recognize that not all feedback may
be constructive or applicable
immediately. Be patient, discerning, and
open to experimenting with different
approaches. This iterative process of
feedback and improvement instills a
culture of continuous learning and helps
ensure that your Raspberry Pi and Python
workshops are always evolving, staying
relevant, and delivering value. It's not
just about teaching, but also about
learning and growing with your
community.

Remember, every step, however small,
taken towards improving your workshop
will ripple out to create a better
learning experience for everyone
involved. So, let's harness the power of
feedback, keep improving, and continue
blazing trails in the world of Raspberry
Pi and Python.

Expanding and Scaling Educational Ventures

Expanding and scaling educational ventures is a process steeped in strategy, creativity, and adaptation. When it comes to Raspberry Pi and Python workshops, consider extending your reach beyond your local community. The rise of online learning platforms and virtual classrooms provides an opportunity to connect with eager learners across the globe. Embrace digital tools that can facilitate interactive and engaging remote learning experiences.

Identify potential partnerships with educational institutions, tech companies, and non-profit organizations that align with your mission. These collaborations can help amplify your reach, provide additional resources, and open up new avenues for growth.

Furthermore, create a comprehensive curriculum that caters to different learning levels — from beginners to advanced learners. Offering specialized modules can attract a wider range of participants and foster a more inclusive learning environment.

Lastly, while scaling up, remain steadfast in preserving the quality of learning. Ensure your expansion plans include mechanisms to maintain, if not enhance, the quality of your workshops. This may involve investing in additional resources or refining your feedback systems.

Scaling educational ventures is a thrilling journey – one that extends the transformative power of Raspberry Pi and Python to more individuals, thereby fostering a globally competent generation of tech enthusiasts.

Monetizing Your Raspberry Pi and Python Workshops

Monetizing your educational workshops requires a strategic approach, a keen understanding of your target audience, and the relentless pursuit of delivering value. To begin with, set a competitive price for your workshops. Conduct market research to understand what other similar workshops are charging and set your prices accordingly. Remember, your prices should reflect the value you're delivering while also covering your operational costs.

Pi Profits

Consider offering tiered pricing to cater to different budgets. For instance, you could have a basic plan for beginners, a premium plan for advanced learners, and even a group plan for educational institutions or companies looking to upskill their workforce.

You could also offer personalized one-to-one coaching sessions for learners who want a more dedicated learning experience. These can be priced higher due to personalized attention and tailored curriculum.

You can monetize further by selling related products or resources. For example, you could develop a detailed guidebook or tutorial videos for Raspberry Pi and Python and sell these online. Or consider creating and selling hardware kits for Raspberry Pi projects. The possibilities are endless.

Another revenue stream could be via affiliate marketing. Partner with retailers selling Raspberry Pi equipment and earn a commission for every sale made through your referral.

Lastly, seek sponsorship from tech companies or grants from educational institutions. In exchange for their financial support, you can offer to display their logo in your workshop materials or give them mentions in your workshops.

Remember, when it comes to monetizing, creativity is your greatest asset. The more value you can provide to your learners, the more opportunities you have to generate income. Always strive to deliver unparalleled learning experiences and the financial rewards will follow.

CHAPTER 5: RASPBERRY PI MEDIA CENTERS

Welcome to Chapter 5: Raspberry Pi Media Centers! In this thrilling part of our journey, we're going to delve into the world of entertainment powered by our tiny titan, the Raspberry Pi. This mighty micro-machine doesn't just excel in the realms of education and tech innovation — it's also a superstar when it comes to leisure and relaxation. You might find it hard to believe, but this pocket-sized computer can transform your humble living room into a multimedia hub, all while leaving your wallet pleasantly unscathed. Whether you're a movie buff, a music aficionado, or a gaming enthusiast, the Raspberry Pi has got you covered. Get ready to explore how this small but mighty dynamo can supercharge your media experiences, turning ordinary nights at home into extraordinary entertainment marvels. Let's dive right in!

Gary Covella, Ph.D.

The Growing Demand for Personalized Media Centers

In the current era of digitization, the demand for personalized media centers is skyrocketing. More and more people are migrating from traditional modes of entertainment towards customized experiences that cater to their specific tastes and preferences. These evolving consumer demands represent a golden opportunity for tech-savvy individuals armed with a Raspberry Pi. With the right blend of creativity and technical know-how, you can transform this mini powerhouse into a full-fledged media center that can stream music, play movies, and even host gaming sessions. This opens up a world of possibilities, allowing you to tailor your entertainment system to match your unique needs and preferences. From customizing playlists to hosting movie marathons, the Raspberry Pi is a game-changer, paving the way for a new era of personalized media consumption.

A Deeper Dive into Kodi and Plex

Both Kodi and Plex are fantastic media center software options that can turn your Raspberry Pi into an entertainment powerhouse. Each software application comes with its strengths, peculiarities, and capabilities, offering unique ways to elevate your multimedia experiences.

Kodi, formerly known as XBMC, is an open-source media player. Its beauty lies in its compatibility with a wide range of operating systems and devices, including our star player, the Raspberry Pi. The highly customizable interface allows you to organize and view your media content in a multitude of ways. Moreover, it supports a plethora of third-party add-ons which can provide access to content from various streaming services. However, remember that some of these add-ons may not be legal, so tread with caution and integrity.

On the other hand, Plex is a media server application that allows you to access your media files from anywhere, as long as you have an internet connection. It organizes your media content into a neat, attractive, and easy-to-navigate interface. The standout feature of Plex is its ability to transcode media files in real-time, ensuring smooth playback on devices with varying capabilities. However, keep in mind that transcoding is a resource-intensive process, and while the Raspberry Pi can handle it, it might struggle with high-resolution files.

In summary, both Kodi and Plex can transform your Raspberry Pi into a personalized media center. Your choice between the two will depend on your specific needs, technical skill level, and the kind of media experience you wish to create. Choose wisely, master its usage, and unlock an unparalleled home entertainment experience.

Setting Up Media Storage Solutions

Media storage is a crucial aspect when it comes to setting up your Raspberry Pi. The device itself may have limited storage, but there are several options available to expand your storage and cater to your needs.

Pi Profits

External Hard Drives

The most straightforward solution to storage concerns is connecting an external hard drive to your Raspberry Pi. With the capability to support up to 2TB (Terabyte) of storage depending upon the model, this option can provide ample space for your media files. Keep in mind, however, that Raspberry Pi lacks the power to run some high-performance hard drives. As such, it's recommended to use a hard drive with its own power source or a powered USB hub.

Network Attached Storage (NAS)

A more advanced option is setting up your Raspberry Pi as a Network Attached Storage (NAS) server. This setup allows the Raspberry Pi to act as a central hub where you can store and access files from any device on your network. In addition to offering a large amount of storage space, a NAS server also provides the convenience of accessing your files from anywhere, anytime.

Cloud Storage

Finally, cloud storage is another viable solution, particularly if you want to access your media files from different locations. Services like Google Drive, Dropbox, and OneDrive can be integrated with your Raspberry Pi. However, remember that while cloud storage is convenient, it relies heavily on your internet connection. Depending upon your bandwidth, streaming high-resolution media from the cloud could be challenging.

In conclusion, there are a variety of media storage solutions available when setting up your Raspberry Pi. Whether you opt for an external hard drive, a NAS server, or cloud storage, each option presents its own set of benefits and drawbacks. The key is to understand your specific requirements and choose a solution that best fits your needs.

Integrating Streaming Services

The advent of the Internet has brought about a sea change in how we consume media. Streaming services like Netflix, Amazon Prime, Hulu, and Disney+ have become go-to sources for movies, TV shows, and documentaries. And guess what? Your Raspberry Pi has the potential to be your new streaming hub.

Kodi: Your Media Center

Let's start with Kodi. A popular open-source media player, Kodi allows you to access and organize your media files conveniently. With its user-friendly interface and compatibility with a wide range of file formats, Kodi is an excellent choice for your Raspberry Pi. You can customize it with a plethora of add-ons to access a variety of streaming services. However, remember that while Kodi itself is legal, accessing copyrighted content without permission is not.

Plex: Stream Your Own Media

Plex is another exciting option for Raspberry Pi enthusiasts. This platform enables you to set up your own personal media server. You can organize your media files, stream them across devices, and even share your library with friends. Plus, Plex offers an intuitive interface and impressive streaming capabilities, meaning you can enjoy your media in high quality, without lag or buffering.

Gary Covella, Ph.D.

<u>Emby: The Plex Alternative</u>

Emby is a media server solution similar to Plex. Emby shines in its customization options and user interface, allowing a personalized viewing experience. Like Plex, Emby also offers live TV and DVR features. However, to unlock its full potential, you'll need to upgrade to Emby Premiere, which costs a bit.

<u>Netflix and Other Streaming Services</u>

Yes, you can watch Netflix on your Raspberry Pi! This involves installing an operating system called OSMC and then running a plugin called PlayOn. This workaround also gives you access to a host of other services like Amazon Prime Video, Hulu, and more. However, this method might not deliver the same streaming quality as watching these services directly from their respective apps.

Remember, the strength of your Raspberry Pi as a streaming hub depends on your specific needs and your willingness to experiment. With the right approach, this tiny computer can become a powerful tool in your media ecosystem. Get creative, try different setups, and play

around until you find the solution
that's just right for you.

Designing a User-Friendly Interface

One of the most critical aspects of your
Raspberry Pi project is the interface.
In an era where user experience reigns
supreme, how your users interact with
the system is of the utmost importance.
A well-designed, user-friendly interface
can enhance the satisfaction of your
users, leading to increased user
engagement and eventually, project
success.

Let's delve into how you can design a
user-friendly interface for your
Raspberry Pi project.

Accessibility and Simplicity

The hallmark of a great interface is its
ease of use. It should be intuitive,
straightforward, and require minimal
instructions. When designing your
interface, keep things simple. Avoid
unnecessary complexities that could
confuse your users. Remember, your
primary goal is to facilitate an
enjoyable user experience.

Gary Covella, Ph.D.

Consistency and Familiarity

Consistency in your interface design is a key factor in the user experience. Users should not have to learn new patterns or navigation methods as they move through your system. The design elements should be consistent in terms of color, typography, and layout. Familiar patterns and layouts help users quickly understand how to interact with your system.

Responsive Design

In today's multi-device world, your interface should be accessible and functional on a variety of devices. Whether it's a desktop, a laptop, a tablet, or a smartphone, your interface should offer the same level of functionality and ease of use.

Feedback and User Communication

Your system should always keep the user informed about what's happening. Whether it's loading, processing, or even an error, immediate and clear feedback can keep users engaged and prevents confusion.

<u>Aesthetics</u>

Finally, the look and feel of your interface can greatly influence user satisfaction. The use of appealing colors, graphics, and typography can enhance the user experience. A visually pleasing interface can often translate to a positive user experience.

By putting the user at the center of your interface design, you can ensure a satisfying experience for your users. Remember, the key to a great user interface is simplicity, consistency, responsiveness, clear communication, and aesthetics. Keep these factors in mind, and your Raspberry Pi project will be a sure-fire hit.

Audio Configurations and Surround Sound

When it comes to audio configurations, the Raspberry Pi proves to be a surprisingly versatile platform. It supports an array of audio outputs, including HDMI, analog stereo audio through the 3.5mm headphone jack, and even digital audio through the I2S interface. This flexibility allows for a wide range of audio projects, from simple music players to complex multi-room audio systems.

The Raspberry Pi also supports a variety of audio formats, including MP3, FLAC, and WAV files. With the right software, it can even function as a full-fledged media server, streaming audio to devices throughout your home or office.

One of the most exciting aspects of audio on the Raspberry Pi is the potential for surround sound. While the Raspberry Pi does not natively support surround sound, it is possible to achieve this with the use of an external audio decoder. Further, the HDMI output can be used to pass through Dolby Digital or DTS audio to your home theater system, enabling high-quality surround sound for your media.

There are numerous software packages available that can help you configure and manage the audio on your Raspberry Pi. These range from simple command-line tools to full-fledged desktop applications, depending on your needs and level of expertise.

The Raspberry Pi's audio capabilities can be extended even further with the use of additional hardware. For example,

DACs (Digital-to-Analog Converters) can be used to improve audio quality, while audio amplifiers can be used to drive larger speakers. Similarly, microphones can be added for recording or voice recognition projects.

In conclusion, the Raspberry Pi's flexible and powerful audio capabilities make it an ideal platform for a wide range of audio projects. Whether you're looking to build a simple music player, a complex home theater system, or anything in between, the Raspberry Pi has you covered.

Case Study: Building a Low-Cost Home Theater

Now, let's delve deeper into our case study: building a low-cost home theater with the power of Raspberry Pi.

Can you imagine firing up your own home theater system that cost less than a dinner for two at a fancy restaurant? Sounds surreal, right? With Raspberry Pi, this dream can soon become your reality.

Start with the Raspberry Pi itself. This tiny board, no larger than a credit

card, serves as the heart of your
budget-friendly home theater. Next,
you'll want to install a suitable
operating system. OSMC (Open Source
Media Center) or LibreELEC are both
excellent choices specifically designed
for home theater setups and are
incredibly user-friendly.

The audio capabilities of the Raspberry
Pi are also worth noting. With the
ability to play a variety of audio
formats, you can enjoy your favorite
tunes in high-quality sound. By using an
external audio decoder, the Raspberry Pi
can replicate a surround sound
experience that rivals many high-end
systems. You can enhance this further by
adding DACs and audio amplifiers to
drive larger speakers, truly packing a
punch in your home theater experience.

Let's not forget about video. With the
ability to support Full HD and even 4K
video streaming, Raspberry Pi ensures
your cinematic experiences are crystal
clear and nothing short of spectacular.

Furthermore, from a software standpoint,
you have options like Plex or Kodi to
manage and stream your media library.
These software packages are highly
customizable, easy to navigate, and can

be remotely controlled from your smartphone, making your movie nights smoother and more enjoyable.

Lastly, remember that the Raspberry Pi comes with connectivity options like Bluetooth and Wi-Fi, so streaming content from your devices or the internet is a breeze.

So, in a nutshell, by using a Raspberry Pi, you are looking at building a versatile home theater system that is light on your pocket but heavy on features. Whether you're a movie buff, a binge-watcher, or just someone who loves a good sound system, embracing the Raspberry Pi for your home theater system can be a game-changer.

Go on then, unleash the tech wizard in you, and assemble an enthralling home theater experience with the magic of Raspberry Pi.

Incorporating Voice and Mobile Controls

Let's dive deeper into the realm of voice and mobile control. Fancy walking into your living room and commanding the lights to dim while your favorite series queues up on Netflix, all with the power of your voice? Well, with Raspberry Pi, this is no longer a distant dream but a reality within your grasp.

Your Raspberry Pi can be integrated with popular AI voice assistants like Amazon's Alexa or Google Assistant. This integration can give you hands-free control over your home theater system, allowing you to play, pause, or search for media with simple voice commands. What's even more fascinating is that you can program custom commands tailored to your movie or music preferences, ensuring a truly personalized touch to your entertainment experience.

Now, for those of you who prefer a more tactile control, Raspberry Pi's compatibility with smartphone apps opens up multiple avenues. By transforming your smartphone into a remote control, you're not just navigating through your media library but also tweaking playback settings, adjusting volume, controlling lights, and even checking on your popcorn in the microwave! This kind of seamless integration between Raspberry Pi and your mobile device makes the smart home experience feel as natural as

flipping through channels on a
traditional TV remote.

Let's remember, the beauty of Raspberry
Pi lies not just in its impressive
capabilities but also in its simplicity
and accessibility. The large community
of Raspberry Pi enthusiasts means you'll
find a wealth of resources and tutorials
online to guide you through each step of
setting up your voice-enabled, mobile-
integrated home theater system. So,
whether you're a seasoned programmer or
a novice taking your first steps in the
coding world, Raspberry Pi ensures that
you have the power to create a tech
marvel within the four walls of your
home.

So what are you waiting for? Gear up,
dive in, and take control - the power of
Raspberry Pi awaits your command. Enjoy
a home theater experience that's truly
your own, crafted by your ideas and
brought to life by this tiny yet mighty
device!

Troubleshooting Common Issues

Before we move any further, let's
address some of the most common issues

that Raspberry Pi users might face when setting up their home theater system. Don't worry, even if you run into these obstacles, it's usually no more complicated than making a good sandwich.

WiFi Connectivity Issues

The first and most common issue is WiFi connectivity. If you're having trouble connecting your Raspberry Pi to your home network, there are a few things you can try. Check whether your router is working properly and your internet connection is stable. Restart your router and your Raspberry Pi. If this doesn't help, make sure you've entered the right network credentials into your Raspberry Pi's settings.

Video Playback Issues

Next, you might experience issues with video playback. Sometimes, videos might not play smoothly, or they might not play at all. This could be due to a number of factors. Check if the video format is compatible with your media player. Another common issue is inadequate power supply, causing the Raspberry Pi to underperform. Use an appropriate power source. If the problem persists, consider upgrading your Raspberry Pi's hardware or software.

Compatibility Problems

Lastly, let's talk about compatibility issues. Raspberry Pi, although impressive, is not immune to compatibility problems with other devices. If your smartphone app isn't syncing with your Raspberry Pi, it could be a problem with the app itself, or it could be due to an outdated operating system on your Raspberry Pi or smartphone. Make sure everything is updated to the latest version.

Remember, folks, building your own smart home theater with Raspberry Pi is like crafting an art masterpiece. It takes patience, creativity, and a bit of troubleshooting. But don't let these minor hiccups discourage you. You're not just creating a home theater system; you're creating an experience, a journey that's as much about the end result as it is about the process. So hang in there, my future tech maestros, your Raspberry Pi masterpiece is just around the corner!

Monetizing Your Raspberry Pi Skills

Let's shift gears for a moment, my tech virtuosos, and talk about turning these Raspberry Pi skills into a money-making machine. Yes, you heard that right, even your home theater project can line your pockets with some serious green.

Firstly, consider offering your services in setting up Raspberry Pi home theaters for others. Not everyone is as technically savvy or as patient as you, and they're willing to pay for a smooth, hassle-free home theater experience. Advertise your services online or locally, and you'll start seeing the dollars flow in.

Secondly, you could start creating and selling custom Raspberry Pi home theater kits. Package together all the hardware, software, and step-by-step instructions needed to build a Raspberry Pi home theater, and you've got yourself a marketable product that caters to the DIY crowd.

Thirdly, if you've got a knack for teaching, why not leverage that? Create a comprehensive online course that takes learners from Raspberry Pi novices to home theater maestros. Platforms like Udemy or Coursera are great places to host your courses, providing you with a built-in audience ready to learn.

And don't forget about affiliate marketing in your instructional content. Whether it's a blog, vlog, or podcast, recommend products that you've used in your Raspberry Pi projects with an affiliate link. Each time a user makes a purchase using your link, you get a small commission. It's like having your cake and eating it too!

Remember, the key to success lies in providing value and solving problems. So, show 'em what you've got, inspire them with your creativity, and the profits will follow.

Here's how you can make money using Raspberry Pi in a step-by-step approach:

Set up Raspberry Pi Home Theaters for Others: Identify your potential clients who lack technical savviness but desire a top-notch home theater. Use online and local platforms to advertise your unique service.

Gary Covella, Ph.D.

Sell Custom Raspberry Pi Home Theater Kits: Gather all the necessary materials, software, and detailed instructions to create a DIY Raspberry Pi home theater kit. Make sure it's accessible and easy-to-follow to attract a wide range of customers.

Develop Comprehensive Online Courses: Are you a good pedagogue? Use platforms like Udemy or Coursera to share your knowledge about setting up a Raspberry Pi home theater. From beginner to advanced levels, cater to all learners who want to master this skill.

Engage in Affiliate Marketing: Alongside your content, be it blogs, vlogs, or podcasts, recommend the products you've used with an affiliate link. Whenever someone purchases through your link, you earn a commission. It's a win-win scenario!

Remember, the secret to success is offering value and problem-solving solutions. Unleash your creativity and the profits will surely follow.

Offering Media Center Customization Services

For those with a knack for customized solutions and a keen eye for detail, offering media center customization services can be a lucrative venture. Raspberry Pi, with its compact size and powerful capabilities, is the ideal platform for such a service.

From Bare Basics to All-Inclusive Luxury

Imagine transforming a simple TV set into a fully-functional, smart entertainment system that can stream movies, play music, and even host video games. This is precisely what you will be doing when you offer Raspberry Pi media center customization services. You can start by offering basic packages where you set up a Raspberry Pi to simply play local media files, then scale up to more advanced packages with network streaming, PVR functionality, and even smart home integration.

Tailor-Made for Every Client

Every customer has unique needs. Some might want a no-frills, easy-to-use setup for their grandparents who are not tech-savvy. Others might want a fully decked-out system with the latest features for their smart homes. With Raspberry Pi, you can customize the media center to suit each customer's requirements perfectly, giving you a competitive edge in the market.

Learning and Upskilling

Setting up a media center with Raspberry Pi involves learning about networking, file systems, and digital media formats. You'll also need to stay updated with the latest technologies and trends in the home entertainment industry. This continuous learning and upskilling not only make the job interesting but also add value to your services.

Building a Brand

As you expand your services and cater to more clients, you'll slowly start to build a brand. Happy customers will recommend your services to others, leading to more business. You could also consider offering after-sales support and updates, further enhancing your reputation and customer loyalty.

Pi Profits

Offering Raspberry Pi media center customization services can be an exciting and profitable venture. Unleash your creativity, offer value, and watch your business flourish.

Gary Covella, Ph.D.

CHAPTER 6: INNOVATING WITH IOT DEVICES

Welcome to Chapter 6, where we'll navigate the exciting world of Internet of Things (IoT) and Raspberry Pi. Just when you thought you had seen it all, this tiny micro-machine reshapes the game, propelling you further into an era of unbounded innovation. In this chapter, we'll delve into how Raspberry Pi is driving the IoT revolution, reinventing the way we connect and interact with devices in our daily lives. From automating your home to optimizing agricultural practices, the possibilities are endless. Buckle up, because you're about to journey into a world where imagination materializes into profitability. Let's dive in!

Introduction to the Internet of Things

The Internet of Things, or IoT, represents a technological revolution. It's the grand network where physical devices around the world connect and communicate through the internet. These devices, embedded with sensors, software, and other technologies, allow for a level of interaction and data exchange like never before. The Raspberry Pi, our versatile microcomputer, acts as a powerful catalyst in this IoT revolution.

The Raspberry Pi's compact size, affordability, and the massive computing power make it a darling for IoT projects. From smart homes to industrial automation, Raspberry Pi is playing a pivotal role in making our world smarter and more connected.

Raspberry Pi and Smart Home Automation

Smart Homes are one of the most visible and exciting applications of IoT, and Raspberry Pi is at the heart of this technology. With Raspberry Pi, homeowners can automate lighting, heating, home security, and even entertainment systems. Imagine walking into your home, the lights automatically adjust to your preference, the thermostat sets just the right temperature, and your favorite music starts playing. All of these are possible with a Raspberry Pi powered smart home.

Raspberry Pi in Agriculture

Agriculture is another sector where Raspberry Pi and IoT are making significant strides. Raspberry Pi can help develop smart farming solutions like precision agriculture and automated irrigation systems. These technologies can monitor soil moisture levels in real-time and automatically trigger irrigation systems based on the data, dramatically improving water efficiency and crop yield.

Raspberry Pi and Industrial Automation

On the industrial front, Raspberry Pi devices are being used for process control and automation, predictive maintenance, and energy management. They help to increase efficiency, reduce costs, and improve safety in the workplace.

In the world of IoT, Raspberry Pi is an essential tool, turning ideas into reality and profit. As you delve deeper into the capabilities of this powerful microcomputer, you'll uncover even more opportunities for innovation and financial gain. The new era of connectivity is here. Embrace it, explore it, and let Raspberry Pi guide your journey into the future of tech innovation.

Advantages of Raspberry Pi in IoT

The Raspberry Pi, in the realm of IoT, is a juggernaut of versatility, accessibility and cost-effectiveness. One of its most profound strengths is its flexibility. This tiny powerhouse is suitable for a wide range of applications, from home automation to industrial control systems. Whether you're aiming to streamline your home's energy use or optimize a factory production line, the Raspberry Pi can adapt to suit a multitude of environments and requirements.

Another compelling advantage of the Raspberry Pi lies in its affordability. As compared to other computing systems, it offers a high performance-to-cost ratio, making tech innovation accessible to more people. This is a major game changer for startups and entrepreneurial individuals who are looking to break boundaries without breaking the bank.

The Raspberry Pi also scores high on user-friendliness. Its open-source nature allows for a wealth of online resources, tutorials, and communities available to assist both novice users and seasoned programmers. You're not merely purchasing a product, but becoming part of a vibrant and supportive ecosystem that can help turn your visions into reality.

Furthermore, the Raspberry Pi's compact size is a boon for IoT applications, where space can be at a premium. Despite its diminutive footprint, it packs in enough power to run multiple tasks concurrently. It's little wonder why the Raspberry Pi has become the go-to choice for many IoT projects.

Lastly, the Raspberry Pi's low power consumption makes it an eco-friendly choice for long-term applications. Especially in IoT deployments, where devices may need to run continuously, the energy-efficient nature of the Raspberry Pi can lead to significant cost savings over time.

Gary Covella, Ph.D.

In conclusion, the Raspberry Pi offers a rich array of advantages for IoT applications. It exemplifies the principle that big things indeed come in small packages. With this microcomputer at your disposal, the bandwidth for innovation widens, paving the way for a more connected and efficient future. Dive into the world of possibilities with Raspberry Pi, and watch it transform your ideas into profitable ventures.

Designing IoT Prototypes

Designing IoT prototypes with Raspberry Pi truly opens up a realm of possibilities. This micro-machine is not just a prototype builder but also an efficient and affordable solution for testing your idea before initiating a large scale production. With Raspberry Pi, you can simulate real-world conditions for your IoT device, making it a cost-effective tool for startups and independent entrepreneurs.

In the world of IoT, communication is key. A Raspberry Pi can be paired with a plethora of sensors and add-on modules, providing the ability to communicate with other devices or the internet.

Pi Profits

These capabilities allow for the creation of complex systems, all controlled from a single Raspberry Pi. From weather stations that tweet their readings, to fully automated smart homes, the humble Raspberry Pi can power it all.

One of the major benefits of Raspberry Pi for IoT projects is its flexibility. With the Raspberry Pi, you're not limited to a specific programming language or operating system. You can use Python, C++, Java, or any other language you're comfortable with. This flexibility allows designers to customize their IoT prototypes to a degree that is not possible with other microcontrollers.

Moreover, the Raspberry Pi offers a robust platform for data processing. Unlike most microcontrollers, the Raspberry Pi is a full-fledged computer with a Linux-based operating system. This means it can run complex software and handle large datasets, making it an excellent choice for IoT applications that require data analytics.

Finally, the vibrant and active community surrounding Raspberry Pi cannot be underestimated. From comprehensive guides to troubleshooters, you'll find a treasure trove of resources to help you at every step. This supportive ecosystem makes the Raspberry Pi an ideal platform for IoT prototyping, helping you turn your entrepreneurial dreams into reality.

In the grand scheme of things, the Raspberry Pi changes the game for IoT prototyping. It's affordable, versatile, and powerful, all while being accessible to both beginners and experienced developers. With this microcomputer in your arsenal, the sky is the limit. So, dive in and start exploring the world of opportunities that Raspberry Pi brings to the realm of IoT.

Taking Advantage of Wi-Fi, Bluetooth, and Zigbee

When it comes to connectivity, Raspberry Pi offers a wide variety of options, making it a highly versatile tool for IoT projects. Let's dive into the three primary connectivity options: Wi-Fi, Bluetooth, and Zigbee.

Pi Profits

Wi-Fi

Most Raspberry Pi models come equipped
with built-in Wi-Fi. This allows your
IoT devices to connect directly to your
home network, or any other Wi-Fi
network, without the need for additional
hardware. What's more, you can leverage
the power of Wi-Fi to connect your
Raspberry Pi to the internet, accessing
online resources and APIs, or even
streaming data to the cloud. This makes
it ideal for IoT applications that
require internet access or need to
handle large amounts of data.

Bluetooth

In addition to Wi-Fi, the Raspberry Pi
also features built-in Bluetooth. This
wireless technology is perfect for
creating local networks of devices.
Bluetooth allows your Raspberry Pi to
communicate directly with other devices
like smartphones, tablets, or other
Raspberry Pis. This is especially useful
in scenarios where you need to control
or get data from other nearby devices.
Think of a smart home system where your
Raspberry Pi controls the lights,
thermostat, and even your TV.

Zigbee

For those who need to go beyond the capabilities of Wi-Fi and Bluetooth, there's Zigbee. Zigbee is a wireless technology that's designed for low-power, low-bandwidth applications. This makes it perfect for IoT applications where devices need to run on battery power for long periods, or where they need to communicate over long distances. Zigbee offers a robust and reliable way to connect your Raspberry Pi to a wide range of sensors and devices.

In summary, the Raspberry Pi offers a plethora of connectivity options to suit any IoT project. Whether you're building a data-intensive application that needs to connect to the internet, a local network of devices controlled by a smartphone, or a power-efficient sensor network, Raspberry Pi has got you covered. So, don't limit your imagination! With Raspberry Pi, you're only limited by the boundaries of your creativity.

Use Case: Smart Plant Watering System

Let's sink our teeth into one of the ingenious applications of the Raspberry Pi: the Smart Plant Watering System. Picture this: you're a busy bee, shuttling between managing your flourishing startup and attending networking dinners. Or you're an enthusiastic traveler, wandering off into the unknown, leaving your beloved greens under the mercy of your unreliable neighbor. Enter the Smart Plant Watering System, your lifesaver, ensuring your green babies thrive, whether you're home or away.

The Raspberry Pi, acting as the brain behind this savvy system, controls the entire process. It connects to various sensors such as soil moisture sensors and water level sensors, gathering data to make informed watering decisions. The soil moisture sensor continuously measures the moisture level in the soil, sending signals to the Raspberry Pi. When the soil is too dry, the Raspberry Pi springs into action and activates the water pump, ensuring your plants get the hydration they need.

The water level sensor, on the other hand, constantly checks the water level in the reservoir. If water levels run low, it signals the Raspberry Pi, which can then send you an automated email or text notification to refill the reservoir. No more worrying about your plants wilting away in your absence.

Moreover, the system can be tweaked and tailored to the specific needs of your plants. Not all plants need the same amount of water, and with the Raspberry Pi, you can adjust the moisture threshold for each plant. You can even schedule watering times or control the system remotely via a web interface.

In essence, the Raspberry Pi empowers you to create a self-sustaining ecosystem right in your living room, backyard, or wherever you choose to place your flora. It promotes plant health, saves water, and gives you peace of mind. So, embark on that impromptu getaway or throw yourself into that demanding project, knowing that your green friends are well taken care of.

What's more, this use case is just the tip of the iceberg when it comes to the potential of the Raspberry Pi. With the Raspberry Pi, the possibilities are as endless as your imagination. So, go ahead and dream big! After all, the world is your oyster when you have a Raspberry Pi in your toolkit.

Use Case: Connected Weather Station

Did you know that you can create your personal, hyper-local weather station right in your backyard, or even on your apartment balcony? Yes, you can! And the Raspberry Pi is the magic wand that can make this happen.

Why settle for generic weather forecasts when you can get real-time data from your surroundings? With a Raspberry Pi connected weather station, you can have access to the most accurate temperature, humidity, and pressure readings directly from your home.

Imagine waking up in the morning, served with the precise weather details right on your phone, smartwatch, or any device of your choice. You get up-to-date observations, enabling you to plan your day better. Deciding what to wear or whether to carry an umbrella becomes a breeze (pun intended). But the magic doesn't stop there.

Gary Covella, Ph.D.

The Raspberry Pi weather station not only measures basic parameters such as temperature and humidity but can also gauge wind speed and direction. If you're an aspiring meteorologist, a gardening enthusiast, or just someone who loves to keep an eye on the weather, this is your golden ticket.

And here's the best part — this station is customizable. You can add a rain gauge or a UV sensor. You can even measure air quality if you are concerned about pollution levels near your home. All this data can be recorded over time, giving you the ability to track changes and patterns directly.

This weather station is definitely not a toy. It is a powerful tool that can match up to commercial weather stations. And all this wouldn't be possible without the versatile, powerful, and compact Raspberry Pi.

So, what are you waiting for? Open the door to a world of meteorological exploration with the Raspberry Pi. Because, why just live under the weather when you can understand it, predict it, and maybe even one day control it?

Security and Privacy Considerations

While the meteorological marvels of Raspberry Pi are undeniably alluring, it's crucial to consider the security and privacy implications of amassing such a wealth of data. After all, in this digital age, any data can be a double-edged sword.

Firstly, it's crucial to ensure the security of your Raspberry Pi weather station. As with any connected device, your weather station could be vulnerable to hacking if not properly protected. Ensure you use strong, unique passwords for all your accounts. Regularly update your passwords and the Raspberry Pi's software to fend off potential security threats.

A firewall is another essential layer of protection. This network security system monitors and controls incoming and outgoing network traffic based on predetermined security rules, acting as a barricade between your trusted internal network and untrusted external networks.

Furthermore, data encryption is an important aspect to consider. Encrypting your data means that even if someone does manage to breach your security measures, they won't be able to make sense of your data without the specific decryption key.

However, security is just one part of the equation; privacy is another. When dealing with weather data, you may be recording and storing a lot of information. While weather data is usually not personal, it still can be used to infer a lot about your living situation, habits, or even your whereabouts. It's crucial that you understand the privacy policies of any third-party platforms or service providers you use to store or analyze your data.

Lastly, consider data minimization — the practice of limiting the amount of data you collect to the bare minimum necessary. This applies to the extent of data you collect, how long you retain it, and who has access to it. By doing so, you reduce the potential for data misuse and enhance your privacy.

Remember, having a Raspberry Pi weather station brings a world of weather data right to your fingertips. But with great data comes great responsibility. Stay smart, stay secure, and respect privacy, and the world of meteorology is yours to explore.

Scaling Production for Commercial Sale

Alright, let's talk about scaling production for commercial sale. It's the point where the rubber hits the road. You've got a killer product - your Raspberry Pi weather station - and you're ready to share it with the world. But to do that, you need to ramp up production.

First thing's first: prototype refinement. Before you even think about large-scale production, you need a final, polished version of your product. This is your golden sample, the model that all your production units will be based on. This stage could involve multiple iterations, extensive testing, and even some late nights, but it's worth it. Because once you have a refined prototype, you know exactly what you're building.

Gary Covella, Ph.D.

Next up: sourcing. You need to identify
reliable suppliers for your components.
This might be a case of simply buying
more Raspberry Pis, or it might involve
sourcing other hardware, like weather
sensors, casing, or even printing
services for your packaging. It's
crucial to find suppliers who can
deliver consistent quality, at a price
that works for your bottom line.

Then, we come to assembly. Depending on
the complexity of your product, this
could be done in-house, or you might
need to outsource to a contract
manufacturer. This is a big decision,
with implications for your cost, quality
control, and lead times. It's worth
taking the time to weigh up your
options.

Last but definitely not least: quality
control and testing. Every unit that
comes off your production line needs to
be tested to make sure it meets your
high standards. This means setting up
processes to check each unit for
defects, functionality, and overall
quality.

Scaling production is no small task.
It's a complex, multi-step process that
requires careful planning, meticulous

134.

attention to detail, and a healthy dose of patience. But when you start seeing your Raspberry Pi weather stations on the shelves, and in the hands of happy customers, you'll know it was all worth it.

Marketing IoT Devices

Unleashing your Internet of Things (IoT) device into the marketplace is an art in itself, a fusion of strategic planning, compelling narratives, and targeted outreach. The first step is understanding your target market. Who are they? What are their needs, their pain points? Why would they be interested in your Raspberry Pi weather station? Answering these questions will allow you to tailor your marketing messages to resonate with potential customers.

Once you've got your target market nailed down, it's time to craft your value proposition. This is your elevator pitch, the thing that sets your product apart from the rest. Maybe it's the precise accuracy of your weather sensors, or the user-friendly interface of your software. Whatever it is, your value proposition needs to be clear, compelling, and prominently featured in all your marketing materials.

Next, consider your marketing channels. These are the avenues you'll use to get your message out to the world. Social media is a powerful tool for reaching a wide audience, especially if you have a visually appealing product. Email marketing allows for more personalized communication, while content marketing-like blog posts, articles, and white papers-can help establish your brand as a thought leader in the IoT space.

However, in the end, all these efforts will fall flat without a strong call to action (CTA). Your CTA is your directive to potential customers, urging them to take the next step. Whether that's pre-ordering a product, signing up for a newsletter, or contacting your sales team for a demo, a compelling CTA is integral to translating interest into sales.

Marketing your IoT device isn't about blasting the world with sales pitches. It's about creating meaningful connections with potential customers, and showing them how your product can add value to their lives. With the right strategy, your Raspberry Pi weather station can become more than just another product on the shelf; it can become a game-changer in the world of IoT devices.

Maintenance and Updates for Users

The process doesn't end once your Raspberry Pi weather station has been purchased and set up by the customer. Maintenance and updates are integral parts of the user's journey and experience with your product.

In a world where technology is evolving at a rapid pace, your weather station isn't immune to this constant change. Regular software updates are crucial for the smooth and efficient operation of your device. These updates not only rectify any bugs or issues but also provide new features and improved functionality that keep your device on par with tech advancements. However, these shouldn't be too frequent or intrusive, as this could interrupt the user's experience and result in dissatisfaction.

Maintenance of your IoT device is another factor that demands your attention. You need to provide your customers with clear, easy-to-follow instructions on how to maintain their device and get the most out of it. This could be through cleaning tips, handling instructions, or troubleshooting guidelines. Remember, customers appreciate it when you make their lives easier.

Moreover, when it comes to IoT devices, security is paramount. Regular updates should also include security patches to protect your device from any potential threats, assuring customers that their data is safe and secure.

Lastly, a strong customer support system is the backbone of a successful IoT product. Provide your customers with ample avenues to reach out—be it through email, phone or social media. A quick, helpful response to their queries or issues can foster trust and loyalty, leading to long-term relationships.

By focusing on maintenance, updates, and customer support, you can ensure your Raspberry Pi weather station remains a valued tool in your customers' lives, rather than a forgotten gadget collecting dust.

Monetizing IoT Devices

So, how do you turn all that expertise into a money-making venture? Here's the big secret: What you're offering here is not just a weather station, but a comprehensive solution. You're selling the peace of mind that comes with accurate weather predictions, the convenience of home automation, and the satisfaction of owning a device that puts power back in the hands of the consumer.

Let's start with the basics: you can sell your Raspberry Pi weather stations directly to the consumers. Craft an enticing sales page that highlights the benefits of owning a personal weather station. Remember, folks aren't buying the gadget. They're buying the idea of a more informed, more efficient, more in-control life.

And don't stop at just selling the device: offer your customers an optional subscription service for regular updates and maintenance. People love convenience and will gladly pay a little extra for a worry-free experience. A subscription model ensures a steady income stream even after the initial sale.

Gary Covella, Ph.D.

You also have the option of creating an instructional course or e-book detailing how to set up, maintain, and make the most of a Raspberry Pi weather station. This not only adds another product to your inventory but also establishes you as an authority in the field.

Finally, consider leveraging affiliate marketing. Use your platform to recommend related products that your customers might find useful—trust me, they'll thank you for it— and earn a commission on each sale made through your referral.

Now, does it require effort? Absolutely. Is it guaranteed to be easy? Absolutely not. But with the right approach and unwavering persistence, you can transform your knowledge into a sustainable, profitable venture.

Follow these steps to capitalize on the Raspberry Pi revolution:

Identify Your Product - First and foremost, decipher what you're offering. Your product here is a Raspberry Pi weather station. Understand what it does and how it enhances the user's life.

Pi Profits

Develop Your Sales Page - Create an enticing sales page that highlights the benefits of owning a personal weather station. Remember to sell the experience and lifestyle, not just the gadget itself.

Create a Subscription Service - Consider offering an optional subscription service for regular updates and maintenance of the weather station. This service should be designed for those seeking convenience and a worry-free experience.

Create an Instructional Course or E-Book - Supplement your product offering by creating a course or e-book that details how to set up, maintain, and get the most out of a Raspberry Pi weather station. This not only adds more depth to your product line but also positions you as an authority in the field.

Leverage Affiliate Marketing - Recommend related products that your customers might find useful. Incorporate affiliate links into your platform and earn a commission on each sale made through your referral.

Persist - Understand that success requires effort and persistence. It

141.

Gary Covella, Ph.D.

might not be easy, but with the right approach and unwavering persistence, you can turn your Raspberry Pi knowledge into a sustainable, profitable venture.

Remember, every step you take brings you one step closer to your entrepreneurial dream. So, go ahead and start your Raspberry Pi journey today!

CHAPTER 7: FREELANCE DEVELOPMENT OPPORTUNITIES

Welcome to Chapter 7 — a treasure trove of information for those seeking to leverage the mighty Raspberry Pi in the world of freelance development. This chapter will guide you on the winding paths of freelance projects, where opportunities are as diverse as they are numerous. From creating intuitive home automation systems to designing immersive gaming experiences or even sculpting digital art installations, the Raspberry Pi is your magic wand. Let's explore how this tiny titan can help you carve a niche in the freelance market, transform your innovative concepts into profitable products, and let you ride the wave of technological revolution. Strap in and prepare to be illuminated.

Gary Covella, Ph.D.

Identifying Market Gaps

Identifying market gaps and capitalizing on them is paramount in the realm of freelance development, especially when you have a versatile tool like the Raspberry Pi at your disposal.

First and foremost, you need to channel your inner explorer. Get curious, and delve into the world of Raspberry Pi applications. Keep your finger on the pulse of the tech industry, and identify areas that are ripe for innovation. Look at existing products and services and think about how you can improve them. Could a Raspberry Pi make a product more efficient? Could it bring down the cost of a service? Could it offer a solution that no one else has thought of? Your unique perspective and innovative approach can uncover opportunities that others have overlooked.

Secondly, don't underestimate the power of networking. Engage with the Raspberry Pi community, both online and offline. Attend industry events, participate in online forums, and connect with like-minded individuals. You never know where your next big idea might come from.

Pi Profits

Then there's the often overlooked, but incredibly valuable process of soliciting feedback. Whether it's from clients, peers or mentors, constructive criticism can help you identify gaps in the market that you may not have noticed. It can also provide invaluable insight into what your potential customers really want and need.

Finally, remember to play to your strengths. If you have a knack for creating visually stunning digital art, consider how you can leverage the Raspberry Pi in this realm. If you're an expert in agricultural tech, think about how this micro-machine could revolutionize the industry. By combining your skills and interests with the capabilities of the Raspberry Pi, you can create unique, in-demand products and services that set you apart in the market.

In the end, identifying market gaps is about thinking creatively, staying informed, and never being afraid to take risks. Now, armed with your Raspberry Pi and imbued with entrepreneurial spirit, it's time to embark on your freelance development journey. Unleash your potential, chase your dreams, and remember — the sky's the limit.

Pitching Raspberry Pi as a Solution

The Raspberry Pi, this little hunk of tech marvel, isn't just a hobbyist's delight, but a bona fide business accelerator. Imagine, for a moment, that you're offering a presentation to potential investors or clients. You don't just waltz in and start blabbering about the Raspberry Pi's potential. No, what you do is pitch it as a solution. And not just any solution, but the solution.

Let's talk about how you could do that. You might start off by painting a picture of the problem — a problem that your audience knows all too well. Maybe it's an issue of cost, or maybe it's about accessibility, or perhaps it's a need for customization. You lay out these pain points, you let your audience feel them, and then — and only then — you introduce the Raspberry Pi.

You tell your audience about this tiny titan of technology, this pocket-sized powerhouse that has the ability to

automate homes, to create immersive
gaming experiences, to drive art
installations and agricultural
innovations. You talk about the
Raspberry Pi not just in terms of what
it can do, but in terms of what it can
solve.

But you don't stop there. You go on to
explain how the Raspberry Pi isn't just
a one-trick pony. It's a platform, a
springboard for innovation. With the
right knowledge and the right approach,
it can be tailored to meet the needs of
a wide range of applications. You
outline the Raspberry Pi's versatility,
its scalability, its potential for
customization - it's not just a product,
it's a toolkit for solving problems.

And then, you wrap up your pitch by
bringing it all back to the audience.
You talk about how they - whether
they're investors, clients, or partners
- can benefit from the Raspberry Pi's
capabilities. Maybe it's about cost
savings, or maybe it's about gaining a
competitive edge, or perhaps it's about
unlocking new opportunities for growth.
You then challenge them to imagine the
possibilities, to envision a future with
the Raspberry Pi at its heart.

147.

Gary Covella, Ph.D.

Pitching Raspberry Pi as a solution isn't just about selling a product. It's about selling a vision, a vision of what could be possible with this remarkable piece of technology in the hands of those who are daring enough, imaginative enough, and ambitious enough to use it. It's about inspiring people to see the Raspberry Pi not just as a tool, but as a catalyst for change.

Effective Communication with Clients

Communicating effectively with clients about the Raspberry Pi begins with understanding their needs, their goals, and their vision. You need to be able to speak their language, to connect with them on their level, and to demonstrate that you truly understand their perspective.

Understand Your Client's Needs

Before you say a word, take a moment to listen. What are they really asking for? What are their pain points? What's their vision for the future? By understanding their needs, you can tailor your message to resonate with them.

Pi Profits

Speak Their Language

When it comes to discussing technical concepts like Raspberry Pi, it's crucial to avoid jargon. Use clear, simple language that your client can easily understand. Remember, you're not trying to impress them with your technical knowledge - you're trying to show them how the Raspberry Pi can solve their problems.

Connect on a Personal Level

While your conversation will ultimately revolve around business, never forget the human element. Show empathy, build rapport, and take an interest in them as individuals. This will make your client feel valued and appreciated, and it will go a long way in building trust.

Demonstrate Your Expertise

While you should avoid technical jargon, that doesn't mean you should shy away from demonstrating your expertise. Use your knowledge to guide the client, to suggest solutions, and to help them see the potential of the Raspberry Pi. Show them you're not just a salesperson - you're a consultant, a partner, a guide.

Gary Covella, Ph.D.

<u>Envision a Future Together</u>

Finally, help your client envision a future where the Raspberry Pi forms an integral part of their operations. Paint a vivid picture of how things could be, of the improvements they could see, of the success they could achieve. Make it tangible, make it real, make it exciting.

Effective communication is about more than simply talking. It's about listening, understanding, connecting, guiding, and inspiring. And when it comes to promoting the Raspberry Pi, it's about opening your client's eyes to a world of possibilities.

Rapid Prototyping for Client Presentations

Rapid Prototyping is an incredibly powerful tool for client presentations, particularly when it comes to showcasing the immense capabilities of the Raspberry Pi. It's not just about telling your clients what this incredible device can do; it's about showing them. Here's how you can use Rapid Prototyping to bring your Raspberry Pi presentations to life.

The Power of Prototyping

Even the most eloquent descriptions can fall short when it comes to conveying the true potential of a technology like Raspberry Pi. This is where Rapid Prototyping comes in. By creating a functional model of your proposed solution, you give the client a concrete demonstration of what's possible. Instead of relying on their imagination, they can see the potential with their own eyes.

The Raspberry Pi Advantage

The Raspberry Pi's small size, affordability, and flexibility make it an excellent tool for prototyping. Whether you're proposing a new IoT application, a custom media center, or a smart home solution, you can build a functional prototype using the Raspberry Pi. This not only brings your presentation to life but also showcases the practicality of implementing your solutions on the Raspberry Pi platform.

From Concept to Prototype

The process of Rapid Prototyping involves taking your solution from an

151.

abstract concept to a tangible model. First, you need to map out your idea, identifying the key features and how they will be implemented on the Raspberry Pi. Then, you'll have to build your prototype. This might involve writing software, assembling hardware, or both.

Showcasing Your Prototype

Once your prototype is ready, it's time to showcase it. During your presentation, demonstrate the functionality of your prototype and explain how it solves the client's problem. Remember to emphasize the cost-effectiveness and scalability offered by the Raspberry Pi. But most importantly, let the prototype speak for itself.

Rapid Prototyping is an excellent way to demonstrate your expertise, connect with your clients, and showcase the potential of the Raspberry Pi. It allows your clients to visualize the future, to see the potential of your solutions, and to understand the power of this tiny yet mighty computer. It is, in essence, the bridge between your client's current situation and the possibilities that lie ahead.

Harnessing the Power of Raspberry Pi in Educational Settings

Imagine a classroom where students are not just consumers of digital technology, but creators and innovators too. Well, that's no longer a figment of imagination, thanks to Raspberry Pi. This little device is a game-changer in the realm of education, providing an affordable, hands-on approach to coding and computational thinking.

In the age where digital literacy has become a sine qua non, Raspberry Pi offers students an opportunity to learn programming languages such as Python, Scratch, and Java. From creating simple code to developing complex programs, students get to understand the nuts and bolts of coding that form the foundation of numerous technologies today.

Beyond coding, Raspberry Pi also enables students to explore hardware. They can learn the workings of a computer, assemble one, and even build devices such as weather stations, radios, or robot cars with this single-board computer. It brings abstract concepts to life, making learning more engaging, practical, and fun.

In addition, the Raspberry Pi fosters creativity and problem-solving skills. Students are encouraged to conceive innovative projects, troubleshoot issues, and develop solutions. It's not just about getting the right answers, but also understanding the process, overcoming challenges, and learning from mistakes. This experiential learning fuels curiosity, resilience, and a growth mindset — invaluable skills for the digital age.

The magic of Raspberry Pi in education extends well beyond the classroom. It's a versatile tool that can also be used for organizing coding clubs, hackathons, and workshops. Moreover, it's a powerful vehicle for bridging the digital divide, providing underprivileged students with access to coding education and digital tools.

In conclusion, Raspberry Pi is transforming education by enabling active, creative, and inclusive learning. With its versatility and affordability, it's democratizing access to digital education, empowering the next generation with the skills they need to thrive in the future. So, whether you're an educator, student, or a tech enthusiast, it's time to explore the potential of Raspberry Pi and revolutionize learning.

Case Study: Custom POS System

Now, let's delve into a real-life application of the Raspberry Pi that has revolutionized the retail industry: the creation of a custom Point of Sale (POS) system.

A POS system is a crucial component of any retail business, handling transactions and managing inventory effectively. Traditionally, POS systems were expensive, bulky, and rigid, offering little flexibility for customization. This is where Raspberry Pi steps in, providing an affordable and customizable solution.

Using the Raspberry Pi, a business owner can create a tailor-made POS system that caters to their specific needs. The system can be equipped with a touch screen for easy operation, a barcode scanner for efficient inventory management, and a receipt printer for customer transactions.

What's more, the Raspberry Pi opens up the possibility of integrating your POS system with other business software. Want to sync your inventory with your online store? No problem. Need to generate sales reports to analyze your business performance? You got it. The Raspberry Pi gives you the freedom to design a system that works for you.

The affordability of the Raspberry Pi also makes it an attractive option for small businesses. Instead of spending thousands of dollars on a commercial POS system, you can build your own for a fraction of the cost. This could be a game-changer for startups and small businesses operating on a tight budget.

Moreover, the Raspberry Pi encourages a DIY approach, allowing you to understand and control every aspect of your POS system. If something goes wrong, you have the knowledge to troubleshoot and fix it, saving you the time and money that would otherwise be spent on professional repairs.

In conclusion, the Raspberry Pi offers a practical and cost-effective solution for businesses looking to modernize their POS systems. It's a perfect example of how this tiny device can be applied in different sectors, empowering entrepreneurs with the tools they need to succeed in the digital age. So, what are you waiting for? Grab your Raspberry Pi and start innovating!

Case Study: Smart Inventory Management

Meet Joe. Joe runs a small hardware store that has been a mainstay of his local community for the past 20 years. But Joe's been having trouble lately. He's been finding it increasingly hard to track his inventory and manage his stock levels efficiently. He's been losing sales because he frequently runs out of popular items. And he's been wasting money because he often overstocks on items that don't sell.

Then, Joe read about our tiny revolutionary computer, the Raspberry Pi. Intrigued by the possibilities, Joe decided to give it a shot. He used a Raspberry Pi to create a smart inventory management system for his store. He attached RFID tags to all his items and set up Raspberry Pi-powered RFID readers at his store entrances and exits. He also set up a Raspberry Pi at his cash register to automatically update his inventory every time a sale was made.

The result? Joe's store has been transformed. His smart inventory system now automatically tracks every item in his store in real time. When a popular item is about to run out, it alerts Joe so he can reorder more. And when an item is not selling, it lets Joe know so he can stop overstocking.

Joe's Raspberry Pi-powered smart inventory management system has not only saved him a ton of time and effort, but it has also significantly increased his sales and reduced his costs. It's made Joe's life a lot easier, and it's made his business a lot more profitable.

And here's the best part: Joe didn't have to spend a fortune to get all these benefits. The Raspberry Pi is an affordable solution that anyone can use. And because it's a DIY solution, Joe was able to tailor his smart inventory system specifically for his store's needs.

So, if you're like Joe and you're looking for a practical and cost-effective way to boost your business, try the Raspberry Pi. With a bit of creativity and innovation, you too can use this tiny device to create big results for your business.

Case Study: Smart Greenhouse Automation

Let's now switch gears and delve into another fascinating application of Raspberry Pi - creating a smart greenhouse system...

Are you an agricultural enthusiast looking to optimize your farming practices? Look no further! The Raspberry Pi is your answer. With its versatile capabilities, it can help you automate and control your greenhouse environment for maximum crop yield.

Imagine having a self-regulating system that constantly monitors temperature, humidity, light levels, and soil moisture inside your greenhouse. That's exactly what the Raspberry Pi can do for you.

With the help of sensors and actuators, you can set up your Raspberry Pi to adjust temperature, humidity, and lighting levels based on predefined thresholds. This eliminates the need for manual intervention, saving you time and labor costs.

Moreover, the Raspberry Pi's data logging capabilities allow you to analyze environmental conditions over time and make informed decisions about when to irrigate, fertilize, or take other necessary actions.

You can also integrate the Raspberry Pi with a mobile app or web interface to remotely monitor and control your greenhouse from anywhere in the world. This gives you more flexibility and convenience in managing your crops.

So why not give it a try? With the Raspberry Pi as your ally, you can create a state-of-the-art smart greenhouse system that maximizes your crop yield and minimizes your efforts. It's time to take your farming game to the next level with this game-changing micro-machine. So, what are you waiting for? Start exploring the endless possibilities of Raspberry Pi today! Stop dreaming big and start making it happen — all thanks to the revolutionary potential of a small computer.

Pi Profits

Keeping Up with Raspberry Pi Development Trends

As you immerse yourself in the world of Raspberry Pi, it is crucial to stay updated with the latest developments and trends. The landscape is always evolving, introducing new software, hardware, and project possibilities that could significantly enhance your entrepreneurial journey.

There are multiple resources available online, including Raspberry Pi's official blog, community forums, and GitHub repositories, where you can find the latest news, project ideas, and code samples. You can also subscribe to Raspberry Pi-focused newsletters or online magazines like The MagPi.

By staying connected with the Raspberry Pi community, you can engage with fellow enthusiasts, learn from their experiences, and even collaborate on exciting projects. You can also get valuable insights into the most common challenges and effective solutions, enabling you to troubleshoot any issues you encounter with your Raspberry Pi projects.

161.

Gary Covella, Ph.D.

So, make it a habit to keep up with the emerging trends and updates. Because in the world of Raspberry Pi, knowledge truly is power — the power to innovate, create, and succeed. Let this dynamic community be your guide on the exciting journey of discovery and innovation you are about to undertake with Raspberry Pi. So, gear up and get ready to ride the wave of progress and opportunities with Raspberry Pi. The only limit is your imagination! Happy tinkering!

Pricing Freelance Services

When it comes to pricing freelance services in the world of Raspberry Pi, determining a fair value can feel like an art. It's a fine balance between charging what you're worth and what the market can bear. As a freelancer, your pricing strategy should not only cover your time and skills but also the value you bring to your clients. Think about it: with Raspberry Pi, you're not just offering a service, you're providing a solution, a way to transform their imagination into reality!

One of the strategies you can adopt is project-based pricing. Instead of charging by the hour, you estimate the entire cost of the project and quote a price upfront. This strategy can be beneficial when dealing with larger, more complex projects where hidden challenges might extend the hours you initially expected.

Alternatively, you can consider an hourly rate. This is often a good approach for smaller projects or when the scope isn't fully defined at the start. To determine your hourly rate, consider factors like your level of expertise, the complexity of the project, and market rates.

Remember, the price you set will reflect the perceived value of your service. So, don't undersell yourself. The world of Raspberry Pi has endless possibilities and a vast audience. Your skillset is unique, and it deserves fair compensation. So, establish your rates, stand by them, and let your work speak for itself.

Building a Portfolio and Client Testimonials

In the world of Raspberry Pi and freelance work, a portfolio showcasing your projects is worth its weight in gold. It is a tangible representation of what you can bring to the table - your skills, creativity, competency, and more. Highlight diverse projects that show versatility and problem-solving abilities. Consider including both completed client work and personal projects that showcase your passion and initiative.

As equally important to your portfolio are client testimonials. They offer social proof, validating your skills and services in the eyes of potential clients. When you complete a project, don't hesitate to ask for a testimonial. Aim for testimonials that speak to the quality of your work, your professionalism, and the value you've provided. These positive reviews can be the deciding factor for potential clients who are on the fence about hiring you.

In sum, when navigating the freelance landscape of Raspberry Pi, a robust portfolio and compelling client testimonials are key assets. They not only increase your credibility but also provide a competitive edge in the marketplace. Remember, people aren't just buying a service; they're buying certainty and confidence in your abilities. So make it a priority to build a portfolio and gather testimonials – they're your freelance passport to success.

Diversifying Your Skillset and Services

To scale your freelance business in the Raspberry Pi landscape, it's imperative to expand your skillset and diversify your service offerings. This tiny computer is a versatile tool, opening avenues for endless applications and innovations. Mastering various software and programming languages linked to Raspberry Pi, such as Python and Scratch, can broaden your market reach. Similarly, familiarize yourself with various Raspberry Pi models and their unique features. This knowledge will empower you to design sophisticated, tailored solutions for your clients.

Additionally, consider venturing into emerging Raspberry Pi applications. From IoT (Internet of Things) to AI (Artificial Intelligence), these high-demand areas present lucrative opportunities.

Gary Covella, Ph.D.

Always remember - the more you learn and adapt, the more valuable you become in this dynamic market. By diversifying your skills and services, you not only future-proof your business but also ensure a steady, growing income stream. Stay curious, stay updated, and keep innovating - that's your mantra for sustained success in the Raspberry Pi freelance world.

CHAPTER 8: DIGITAL ART INSTALLATIONS AND INTERACTIVITY

In Chapter 8, we're going to delve into an exciting arena where technology meets creativity - Digital Art Installations and Interactivity. Raspberry Pi has been a game-changer in this domain, offering artists a dynamic canvas to express their creativity while stirring audience interactivity. Not only does this empower artists to transcend traditional boundaries, but it also paves the way for entrepreneurs to tap into profitable ventures. So, whether you're an art aficionado looking to revolutionize your aesthetic expressions, or an entrepreneur seeking unique business opportunities, this chapter will equip you with the knowledge and tools to harness the power of Raspberry Pi in the realm of digital art installations. Let's get started on this fascinating journey where art meets code!

Gary Covella, Ph.D.

The Convergence of Art and Technology

Art and technology might seem like two separate entities, but they've been intertwining more and more, giving birth to an entirely new realm of possibilities. The burgeoning field of digital art installations is one fine example of this convergence. With a tiny computer like Raspberry Pi at the core, artists are now equipped with the power to create interactive installations that not only captivate audiences but also immerse them in the experience. The use of Raspberry Pi in these art installations has opened up a myriad of opportunities, enabling artists to bring their visions to life in ways that were previously unimagined. By leveraging the power of this micro-machine, artists can now create dynamic displays that respond to external stimuli in real time, creating a two-way interaction between the viewer and the art piece. The blend of art and technology has not only expanded the horizons of artistic expression, but also created new avenues for entrepreneurs to venture into. With the right knowledge and tools, one can capitalize on this emerging field and open doors to a host of profitable opportunities.

Planning and Sketching Digital Installations

Before diving headfirst into creating a digital installation, it's essential to begin with a solid plan. Sketching out your ideas on paper may seem archaic in this digital age, but it's a powerful way to visualize and refine your concepts. Think about the components you'll need to bring your vision to life. Consider the size, location, and environment of your installation. How will viewers interact with your piece? If your project uses sensors, decide on their placement to ensure optimal interaction. You'll also want to contemplate your Raspberry Pi's capabilities. While it's a versatile tool, it does have limitations. Balancing your grand artistic vision with the practicalities of your hardware is a vital part of the planning process. This preliminary step of sketching and planning is the foundation upon which successful digital installations are built. This is not just about creating art; this is about choreographing an experience that resonates with viewers.

169.

Gary Covella, Ph.D.

And remember, this journey is as much about problem-solving and improvisation as it is about creativity. So, let your imagination run wild, but always stay grounded in the practicalities of your digital toolkit.

Raspberry Pi in Interactive Art: Potential Use Cases

The Raspberry Pi's potential in interactive art is vast and captivating. Imagine a digital art piece that mirrors the viewer's emotions by changing colors or patterns in response to detected facial expressions. Or consider an interactive sound installation that changes its melody based on the proximity and movement of the audience. Such dynamic, immersive experiences can be crafted using the Raspberry Pi's power to process inputs from cameras, microphones, or sensors and output through screens, speakers, or LED lights.

Moreover, Raspberry Pi can breathe life into static artwork. Consider a traditional painting rigged with a Raspberry Pi and a small screen. The screen could periodically change to reveal hidden layers of the painting or

170.

reveal the artist's comments on the piece. This fusion of classical and digital art could introduce a new layer of depth and interaction to the viewer's experience.

Finally, the Raspberry Pi's networking capabilities open a world of possibilities for collaborative and distributed artworks. Multiple devices can work together to create a large, connected display, or participate in a shared online art project. These are just the tip of the iceberg when it comes to the potential use cases of Raspberry Pi in interactive art. So, step into this captivating world and let your creativity soar!

Integration with Sensors for Interactive Displays

Building on the Raspberry Pi's potential in interactive art, we can delve further into its relationship with various sensors for creating interactive displays. Raspberry Pi can integrate with a wide array of sensors such as temperature, humidity, motion, light, sound, and many more. These sensors can be used to gather real-time data, providing the building blocks for a truly interactive art experience.

For instance, think about a visual art display that changes depending on the ambient temperature or light level. As the day transforms from dawn to dusk, your art installation can mirror the mood, evolving in color, pattern, and intensity. Such dynamic interaction can transcend the boundaries of traditional static art, making the viewer an integral part of the creation process.

Furthermore, imagine a sound installation that reacts to movements of visitors. As people move around the space, their actions could trigger different sounds, melodies, or rhythms, creating an ever-changing and unique auditory experience. The possibilities are as limitless as your imagination, and the Raspberry Pi is your magic wand, ready to transform ordinary materials into interactive art pieces. So, gear up and let's dive deeper into the world of sensor-integrated interactive displays with Raspberry Pi!

Case Study: Raspberry Pi-Powered Light Show

In the bustling city of Tokyo, an innovative artist, Hiroshi Jacobs, has taken Raspberry Pi-integrated art to new heights. Jacobs, known for his immersive installations, created a groundbreaking light show entitled 'Illuminosity.' This installation was unique in that it used a Raspberry Pi to control an array of LED lights, creating a spectacle of colors and patterns that enthralled viewers.

'Illuminosity' was set up in a public park, blending technology and nature in a harmonious dance of light and color. The Raspberry Pi was connected to a multitude of sensors placed strategically across the park. These sensors collected data such as temperature, humidity, light levels, and even the movement of people and animals in the vicinity. This data was then processed by the Raspberry Pi, which adjusted the patterns, colors, and intensity of the LED lights in real-time.

The result was an ever-evolving light show that responded to the environment

173.

and the presence of viewers, offering a truly interactive experience. As people moved through the park, their motion changed the patterns of light. Even the time of day or weather conditions impacted the light show, creating a continuously shifting display of art.

The success of 'Illuminosity' is a testament to the immense potential of integrating Raspberry Pi with sensors for creating interactive displays. It underscores the idea that technology, when synergized with art, can create experiences that are immersive, engaging, and above all, unique. Now, it's your turn to harness the power of Raspberry Pi and sensors, and create your own masterpiece.

Case Study: Interactive Soundscapes

Taking inspiration from 'Illuminosity,' a group of sound artists decided to go a step further by integrating Raspberry Pi with sound. They developed an interactive soundscape project titled 'Audible Echoes.' This project was situated in a bustling urban park and sought to create a serene auditory oasis amidst the city's cacophony.

Pi Profits

In 'Audible Echoes,' multiple sensors were placed around the park, collecting data ranging from weather conditions to the intensity of pedestrian traffic. The Raspberry Pi processed this data in real-time to produce a dynamic soundscape that reflected the park's environmental and human activity. If the park was busy, the soundscape might have been a symphony of birdsong or a gentle rainfall to soothe the listeners. In contrast, a quiet, rainy day might trigger a soft melody or an inspiring musical piece.

As with 'Illuminosity,' the beauty of 'Audible Echoes' lay in its interactivity. The soundscape responded not just to environmental stimuli, but also to the presence and movement of listeners. As visitors moved through the park, the sounds around them changed, creating a unique auditory journey for each individual.

The success of 'Audible Echoes' illustrates the potential of Raspberry Pi for interactive sound art. By harmonizing technology, art, and environment, it's possible to generate immersive experiences that engage people in new and surprising ways. So, are you

ready to let your imagination run wild
and create your own interactive
soundscape with Raspberry Pi? Your next
profitable venture could be just a
melody away.

Showcasing Art: Galleries vs. Public Spaces

When it comes to showcasing art, the
choice between galleries and public
spaces can significantly influence the
interaction dynamics between the
audience and the artwork itself.
Galleries, traditionally known for their
controlled environments, offer a serene
and focused setting. This allows the
audience to appreciate each piece in
isolation, without any distractions.
However, this also confines the art
within the four walls of the gallery,
limiting its reach to only those who
intentionally visit it.

On the other hand, public spaces provide
an open canvas that invites a broader
and more diverse audience. Art in public
spaces integrates itself into the daily
life of people, creating a spontaneous
and dynamic interaction. This is where
Raspberry Pi powered installations like
'Audible Echoes' truly shine. They bring

art to people's everyday life, transforming mundane spaces into immersive, interactive experiences. Using Raspberry Pi, artists can turn a bustling park, a lonely alleyway, or even a drab office building into a vibrant art installation, providing a unique blend of art and daily life. This democratic approach to art not only fosters a heightened sense of community but also opens up avenues for more innovative and profitable ventures.

Collaborating with Artists and Creators

Artists and creators seeking to broaden their horizons have an invaluable tool in Raspberry Pi. This tiny yet powerful device is capable of transforming simple ideas into captivating, interactive installations. Its versatility allows for a myriad of collaborations across disciplines, from musicians and digital artists to game developers and educators. These collaborations not only bring forth a fusion of diverse skills and perspectives but also pave the way for unique, innovative creations that were previously unthinkable. For instance, a musician could team up with a coder to create interactive

177.

soundscapes that react to audience movements, while a digital artist could work alongside an engineer to create kinetic sculptures controlled by custom software. The possibilities are endless with Raspberry Pi, opening up new avenues of expression, creativity, and yes, profitability. So grab your tool-kit, rally your team, and let Raspberry Pi guide you on an entrepreneurial journey of innovation and artistry.

Maintenance and Longevity of Digital Installations

With the correct handling and maintenance, your digital installations can enjoy an extended lifespan, providing your audience with an immersive experience for years to come. Raspberry Pi, a robust and reliable device, is designed to withstand the test of time. But like any other piece of technology, it requires care and attention to ensure it continues to function optimally. Regular software updates, for example, are crucial for maintaining the device's performance and security. Aside from software upkeep, it's also essential to consider the physical aspects of maintenance. Keeping your Raspberry Pi dust-free, ensuring it's housed in a suitable case, and protecting it from extreme temperatures, can all contribute to its longevity. By taking these steps, you're not just prolonging the life of your device — you're also ensuring that your digital art installations continue to engage and inspire, enhancing the everyday lives of those who encounter them.

Monetizing Art: Sales, Exhibitions, and Sponsorships

Creating art with Raspberry Pi is not just a creative journey, but can also be a smart financial move. As an artist, you can profit from your creations in various ways. Selling your pieces outright is the most apparent income stream, but it's not the only one. Consider holding exhibitions — these not only work as a platform to showcase and sell your work but can also attract media attention, boosting your profile in the industry. Sponsorships can be another significant source of revenue. Tech companies, intrigued by the innovative use of Raspberry Pi in artistic expressions, may sponsor your art installations. This mutually beneficial alliance can provide you with the necessary funds to create your art,

179.

Gary Covella, Ph.D.

while the company gains exposure from
being associated with your work.
Remember, your creativity, coupled with
strategic monetization, can turn your
passion into a viable income source.

Profit-Making with Pi: A Step-By-Step Guide

Create Your Raspberry Pi Art Project:
The first step to monetizing your
creativity is to create an art piece
with your Raspberry Pi. Use your unique
artistic vision to create a piece that
not only showcases your skills but also
highlights the capabilities of this
potent micro-machine.

Showcase Your Work: Once your art piece
is ready, it's time to showcase it. Hold
exhibitions to display your project to
the public. This will not only help you
sell your pieces but also attract
valuable media attention, amplifying
your visibility in the industry.

Explore Sponsorship Opportunities: Reach
out to tech companies and propose a
sponsorship. Art installations that
leverage Raspberry Pi are likely to
pique their interest. This could
potentially result in a mutually

beneficial alliance where they provide
you with funds and in return, receive
publicity from being associated with
your innovative project.

Sell Your Art: Direct selling of your
art pieces is also a practical income
stream. Remember to price your work
appropriately, considering not just the
cost of materials, but also the time,
skill, and creativity that went into it.

Repeat: Keep innovating and creating new
art installations. The more you create,
the more opportunities you'll have to
sell, attract sponsors, and boost your
profile in the art and tech industry.
Always remember, continuous creativity
is the key to sustainable income in this
field.

Gary Covella, Ph.D.

CHAPTER 9: ENHANCING NETWORKS WITH PI-HOLE

Welcome to Chapter 9, where we will tackle the intriguing world of network enhancements with Pi-hole. As we journey further into the multifaceted uses of Raspberry Pi, we delve into its use in network management. You might wonder, 'What is Pi-hole?' Simply put, it's a network-wide ad blocker. But it's more than just that. It's a doorway to a clutter-free, secure, and smooth browsing experience. In this chapter, we'll unfold how you can use the Raspberry Pi to set up a Pi-hole, enhancing your network by minimizing unwanted ads and protecting your data. If you've ever been irked by intrusive ads or concerned about online privacy, this chapter is your ticket to a cleaner, safer, and faster internet experience. Buckle up, because we're about to step into a browsing renaissance!

Gary Covella, Ph.D.

Understanding Digital Advertising and Trackers

Digital advertising has become an integral part of the internet. Every time we browse a webpage, use a social media platform, or engage with an online service, we're likely to encounter numerous digital ads. These ads help keep many of our favorite web services free, but there's a downside. Advertisers often deploy tracking technology to monitor your online behavior. These trackers collect information about the sites you visit, the products you view, and even how long you spend on each page. This data is then used to build a profile of your interests, which advertisers use to target you with personalized ads. While some see this as a harmless way to deliver more relevant advertising, others view it as an intrusion of privacy. This is where tools like Pi-hole come into play, blocking ads and trackers network-wide, which in turn enhances your browsing speed and protects your online privacy.

184.

Introduction to Network-Level Ad Blocking

Pi-hole, a powerful open-source software run on a Raspberry Pi, operates at the network level, meaning it's capable of blocking ads across all devices connected to the same network. From smartphones to smart TVs, any device that's part of your network can benefit from this ad-blocking power. Imagine browsing without annoying pop-ups, interruptive banner ads, or hidden trackers - that's the experience Pi-hole offers.

Not only does it eliminate ads, but it also significantly speeds up your internet. By blocking ad requests at the onset, websites load faster, resulting in a smoother, more efficient online experience. Furthermore, it curbs the stealthy data harvest by tracking technologies, thereby enhancing your online privacy.

So how does it accomplish all this? Pi-hole works by acting as your network's DNS server. When a device in your network requests a webpage, Pi-hole steps in. It checks the requested site against a regularly updated list of ad-serving domains. If it finds a match, Pi-hole blocks the request, meaning the ad never loads on your device. The result? An ad-free, privacy-focused browsing experience for all your network's devices, thanks to the humble Raspberry Pi and the powerful Pi-hole software.

Setting Up Pi-hole: A Step-by-Step Guide

Before diving into the setup process, it's important to understand the prerequisites. You will need a Raspberry Pi with an installed operating system (Raspbian is the most popular choice), a stable internet connection, and a bit of patience to follow through the steps meticulously.

Required Hardware and Software

Raspberry Pi (Any model with an Ethernet/WiFi connection will do, but the Raspberry Pi 3 Model B or newer is ideal)

SD card (8GB or larger)

Ethernet cable or WiFi connection

Pi Profits

A copy of the Raspbian operating system

Power supply

Installation Steps

Setting up the Raspberry Pi: Firstly, you need to have your Raspberry Pi ready to go. This means it should have Raspbian installed, and be connected to your network. Once you are logged in to your Pi, ensure it's up to date by running the following commands in the terminal:

```
```

sudo apt-get update

sudo apt-get upgrade

```
```

Installing Pi-hole: Now that your Raspberry Pi is ready, the next step is to download and install Pi-hole. In the terminal, simply write the following command and hit Enter:

```
```

curl -sSL https://install.pi-hole.net | bash

187.

` ` `

The installer does all the work, setting up Pi-hole to run in the background as a daemon, where it can monitor all your network traffic.

Future chapters will delve into the intricacies of customization, optimization, and possible challenges you might encounter during the process, and how best to troubleshoot them. Stay tuned as we unravel the power and potential of Raspberry Pi and Pi-hole to redefine your digital life.

Customizing Blocklists

Customizing blocklists is where the true power of Pi-hole comes into play. This is your fortress, your digital kingdom, and you decide who's allowed in. Customizing blocklists is about taking control of your browsing experience. It's about deciding what's relevant, what's intrusive, and what's downright annoying. It's about reclaiming the internet as a tool for your use, not the other way around.

Pi-hole comes with a default blocklist that's pretty comprehensive, but let's face it, the internet is a big place and some ads are sneakier than others. Each individual's browsing habits are unique, and that means what you consider to be an annoyance may not be the same for someone else. Thankfully, Pi-hole allows you to add and remove websites from your blocklist as you see fit.

In the following chapter, we're going to walk you through how to fine-tune your blocklists to create the most seamless browsing experience possible. So buckle up, because we're about to take a deep dive into the world of Pi-hole customization. Stay with me and discover how to make the internet bend to your will. More power to you, my friend!

Monitoring Network Activity and Queries

Monitoring your network activity is not just about keeping an eye on the data usage but having a detailed overview of what's going on in your digital kingdom. Pi-hole provides real-time, detailed insights into your network activity with its built-in web interface. This is your watchtower, providing you a bird's eye view of all the requests coming in and going out of your network.

Not only does Pi-hole show you the total number of queries made, but it also breaks it down into what was allowed and what was blocked. It's quite satisfying, let me tell you, to see the number of ads you're stopping in their tracks. Like a night watchman, the Pi-hole logs every query, so you can analyze the traffic and adjust your blocklists accordingly.

But Pi-hole doesn't stop there. It also offers a unique feature - the top permitted and top blocked domains. This gives you an idea about the most frequented websites and the most intrusive ones. Being informed is being empowered, and Pi-hole ensures you are that. So, ready to step into your watchtower and wield the power of knowledge? The next chapter will guide you on how to use the Pi-hole web interface to monitor your network activity. Stay tuned, there's much more to explore!

Ensuring Smooth Internet Experiences for Users

When it comes to internet experiences, nobody likes disruptions or slow-downs. Particularly not when you're in the

middle of something important or really
deep into a gripping series. That's
where Pi-hole steps in to ensure smooth
sailing. It's not just about blocking
ads, it's about enhancing your internet
experience, making it more streamlined
and less cluttered.

Pi-hole ensures that the ads do not
consume a significant portion of your
bandwidth. By blocking them at the DNS
level, it prevents them from ever
reaching your network, freeing up your
bandwidth for the stuff you really care
about. This means your pages will load
faster, and your video streams will be
less likely to buffer.

But it's not just about speed. Pi-hole
also gives you control over what content
is allowed on your network. You can
create whitelists for the websites you
trust and want to support, and
blacklists for those you'd rather avoid.
This way, you can customize your online
environment to suit your preferences,
ensuring a more enjoyable, and safe,
internet experience.

Stay with me, we've only just begun to
unveil the potential of Pi-hole. In the
next chapter, we'll dive deeper into the
waters of customization. Strap in for

191.

the ride and get ready to seize control of your online world!

Security and Privacy Enhancements

In this digital age, where privacy seems to be a luxury, Pi-hole serves as a veritable fortress, safeguarding your online data from those prying eyes lurking in the shadows of the internet. Imagine a world where you're invisible to the countless data collectors that stalk your every click, seeking to profile you for their benefit. That's the world Pi-hole offers.

By blocking trackers at the DNS level, Pi-hole prevents these data collectors from ever getting a whiff of your online activities. It's like having a personal bodyguard who ensures that you can browse in peace, free from the anxiety of being watched and profiled. But that's not all. Pi-hole also protects you from malware and phishing attempts, further enhancing your online safety.

Pi-hole's commitment to privacy does not stop at blocking trackers and ads. The tool respects your privacy and does not log your DNS queries. So not only are you invisible to the data collectors, but you're also invisible to Pi-hole!

In the next chapter, we'll reveal how to fine-tune your Pi-hole to offer maximum protection for your network. So, stick around! The journey towards a safer, more private internet experience is just heating up!

Offering Installation as a Service

In this ever-evolving technological landscape, one of the most promising endeavors is offering Pi-hole installation as a service. With an increasing number of users recognizing the manifold benefits of Pi-hole, the demand for experts who can seamlessly set it up is on the rise.

Selling your expertise in Pi-hole installation is akin to selling peace of mind. You are not merely setting up a tiny device; you are erecting a robust shield that defends users against the incessant onslaught of unwanted ads, invasive trackers, and malicious content. Imagine being the sentinel who safeguards users' browsing experience, ensuring they can navigate the vast terrain of the Internet, unimpeded and unobserved.

But before you jump into this venture, you must master the art of Pi-hole installation. Knowledge is your most potent tool. The more adept you become, the more value you can offer to your clients, and the more profitable your service will be.

In the following chapters, we'll equip you with the skills and strategies you need to turn Pi-hole installation into a lucrative business. So stick around, because the real journey is just about to begin!

Maintenance and Updates for Clients

Beyond the installation, your clients will undoubtedly need ongoing support to keep their Pi-hole systems running smoothly. That's where your services for maintenance and updates come in. As a Pi-hole expert, you'll need to keep an eye on updates, bug fixes, and possible system enhancements, ensuring that your clients always have the latest and greatest version of their Pi-hole system.

Additionally, clients may encounter complexities that go beyond their comprehension. In such scenarios, your expertise will be their lifeline. Whether it's a malfunctioning network, a stubborn ad slipping through the defenses, or an inexplicably slow Internet speed, you'll be there to troubleshoot and set things right. Offering these services not only adds a steady income stream but also helps forge long-term relationships with your clients, who will appreciate your in-depth knowledge and prompt assistance.

As you dive deeper into maintenance and updates, remember that your role isn't just that of a technician but also a mentor. Educate your clients about the importance of regular updates and system checks, and how it plays a pivotal role in ensuring their digital safety. As always, knowledge is power, and by sharing it, you're empowering your clients while cementing your role as their trusted guide in the world of Pi-hole. Stay tuned, as the next chapter will delve into strategies for effective client communication and education.

Gary Covella, Ph.D.

Expanding Services: Beyond Ad-Blocking

Don't get it twisted folks, Pi-hole is not just an ad-blocking gizmo; it's a damn gold mine of entrepreneurial opportunities! Let me tell you, the world of Pi-hole goes way beyond blocking those pesky pop-ups. This wonderful little black box can perform a range of services that can add some serious numbers to your bottom line.

Let's say you've got a client who's a stickler for privacy. With a few tweaks, Pi-hole can double up as a local DNS resolver, adding an extra layer of privacy protection. Or maybe you've got a client running a home office or a small business, who needs a reliable and affordable network monitoring solution. Guess what? Pi-hole can do that too!

And here's where it gets really interesting. As an entrepreneur, you can offer these additional services to your clients at a premium. It's a win-win situation. Your clients get the benefit of an enhanced Pi-hole system, and you get the benefit of increased revenue. So, step out of the ad-blocking box and start exploring the endless

196.

possibilities that Pi-hole has to offer. Trust me, there's gold in them hills!

A Step-by-Step Guide to Turn Pi-hole into a Money-Making Machine

Let me break this down for you, people, so you can start carving out your piece of that Pi-hole gold!

Identify the need: Figure out what your clients, or potential clients, truly need. Are they fed up with invasive ads? Concerned about online privacy? Or maybe they're looking for an affordable network monitoring solution? Once you know what they want, you can start tailoring your Pi-hole services to meet these needs.

Customize your Pi-hole services: Offer more than just ad-blocking. Turn Pi-hole into a local DNS resolver for those who value privacy, or transform it into a network monitoring tool for home offices and small businesses. The key is to expand your services beyond what people initially expect.

Set your rates: Remember, you're providing a premium service here, so

price it accordingly. Don't sell
yourself short. You've found a solution
to your clients' problems and that adds
value.

Promote your services: Get the word out,
people! Use your website, social media,
newsletters, and word-of-mouth referrals
to promote your enhanced Pi-hole
services. Let your clients know how you
can help them with more than just ad-
blocking.

Deliver excellent service: This is where
the rubber meets the road. Make sure you
deliver top-notch service and support.
Remember, a happy client is a repeat
client, and they'll likely refer you to
others as well.

Rinse and repeat: The beauty of this
process is that it's repeatable. As you
gain more experience and feedback, you
can continue to refine and expand your
services. You'll be sitting on a
mountain of gold before you know it!

Remember folks, opportunity doesn't
knock twice. It's time to roll up your
sleeves and start turning that Pi-hole
into a profit machine. The gold rush is
on, will you strike it rich?

CHAPTER 10: PRE-CONFIGURED RASPBERRY PI KITS

In the tenth chapter, we'll dive into the realm of pre-configured Raspberry Pi kits. If you're looking to bypass the fuss of setting up from scratch, then these kits are your golden tickets. They bundle together all the essential components, and often toss in a few extras, offering a ready-to-launch platform for your ideas. Ideal for beginners and convenient for seasoned pros, these kits are gateways to swift innovation. Let's set sail into this exciting chapter and get a glimpse into the world of Raspberry Pi kits that are just waiting for you to plug in and play.

Importance of DIY Kits in Learning

DIY Kits are integral to the learning process, particularly when it comes to technology like Raspberry Pi. They serve as a tangible, hands-on approach to learning that fosters a deeper understanding of concepts and promotes creative problem-solving. By providing all the necessary components in one package, these kits enable learners to focus more on exploration and less on sourcing materials. Furthermore, they offer a sandbox-like environment where learners can experiment, make mistakes, and learn by doing, which is a cornerstone of effective learning. So whether you're a seasoned techie or a beginner, a DIY Raspberry Pi kit can offer valuable learning experiences that can fuel your passion for technology and innovation.

Identifying Trending Raspberry Pi Projects

Riding the wave of popular Raspberry Pi projects is a sure-fire way of staying relevant in the ever-evolving tech landscape. Whether you're a hobbyist or a professional, staying in sync with the latest trends can provide inspiration for your next big project. Some trending applications include retro gaming consoles, home automation systems, weather stations, and even AI-powered robots.

Retro Gaming Consoles

A nod to the past, building retro gaming consoles with Raspberry Pi has garnered significant attention. By using emulators, these consoles can replicate the experience of classic gaming systems, transporting gamers back in time while offering a do-it-yourself satisfaction.

Home Automation Systems

Raspberry Pi is also making waves in the home automation arena. From managing lighting systems to regulating temperature controls, Raspberry Pi-driven home automation projects are transforming everyday living, making it more convenient and energy-efficient.

Weather Stations

Weather enthusiasts are exploiting Raspberry Pi's potential by creating personal weather stations. These stations can monitor local weather conditions, providing real-time data on parameters like temperature, humidity, and pressure.

Gary Covella, Ph.D.

AI-Powered Robots

The marriage of Artificial Intelligence (AI) and Raspberry Pi has given birth to a new breed of AI-powered robots. These robots can perform a myriad of tasks, from voice recognition to object detection, opening up fascinating avenues in the field of robotics.

By identifying and exploring these trending projects, you can keep your finger on the pulse of the Raspberry Pi world, ensuring you're never left behind in this fast-paced realm of innovation.

Sourcing Components and Ensuring Quality

When diving into a Raspberry Pi project, sourcing quality components is of paramount importance. Components form the backbone of your project, and their quality directly impacts the performance and longevity of your Raspberry Pi system.

You can purchase components from a variety of online and physical stores; however, it's important to select reputable suppliers. Research customer reviews and ratings to gauge the reliability and quality of the products. While it may be tempting to latch onto the cheapest deal, remember that quality often comes at a price.

In terms of hardware, you'd need a Raspberry Pi board, SD Card for storage, power supply, and depending on your project, you might need additional components such as sensors, cameras, or LED displays. When it comes to software, Raspberry Pi supports various open-source operating systems; the choice of which depends on your project demands and personal preference.

Remember, your Raspberry Pi set-up is only as strong as its weakest link. Therefore, ensuring each component is top-notch will set you on the path to a successful project. So, go ahead and roll up your sleeves, embark on this journey of discovery and innovation, and let Raspberry Pi unlock a whole new world of opportunities for you.

Designing an Engaging Instruction Manual

Creating an engaging instruction manual for Raspberry Pi is akin to crafting a roadmap for innovation. The manual should be comprehensive yet easy to understand, guiding both beginners and experienced users through the captivating world of Raspberry Pi. The first step in this journey is to lay a solid foundation. Explain the basics of the Raspberry Pi system, its components, setup processes, and the numerous possibilities it offers. Treat the user not just as a reader, but as an explorer poised to discover the vast potential of this tiny yet potent computer.

The manual should also house a blend of easy and complex projects, with detailed, step-by-step instructions and illustrative diagrams to facilitate understanding. It's also crucial to highlight common pitfalls and troubleshooting methods to help users navigate challenges. Including real-world examples and success stories can serve as a motivational boost, demonstrating the practical application and potential profitability of Raspberry Pi projects.

Finally, make the manual interactive and exciting. Encourage users to experiment, tweak and customize their projects, fuelling their creativity and entrepreneurial spirit. Remember, in the realm of Raspberry Pi, the only limit is one's imagination. So, gear up to craft a manual that not only instructs but also inspires, paving the way for the next generation of innovators.

Packaging: Aesthetics and Unboxing Experience

When it comes to packaging your Raspberry Pi kit, aesthetics, and the unboxing experience matter. It might seem like an afterthought, but packaging is a significant part of the customer's journey, and it deserves your attention. The unboxing moment is a tactile and visual interaction with your product, and you want your customers to feel the excitement and anticipation that comes with unraveling a new gadget.

A well-thought-out package design doesn't just protect the product inside; it tells a story. It could be an expression of your brand, a clue about the product within, or even a hint of the treasure trove of possibilities that the small Raspberry Pi holds. Use vivid colors, imaginative fonts, and engaging visuals to create a package that's not just a container, but a conversation starter.

Gary Covella, Ph.D.

Inside the box, neatly layout all components, maybe even grouped based on the assembly sequence. Remember, the aim is to make the setup process as intuitive as possible. Include a printed version of the quick-start guide or a link to an online setup video. This takes the guesswork out of the assembly process and makes it accessible to users of all skill levels.

Lastly, don't shy away from adding a personal touch. A thank-you note, a fun sticker, or even a quirky Raspberry Pi-themed collectible can make the unboxing experience memorable. It's these little details that make a product stand out, creating a lasting impression in the minds of your customers.

Setting Up Support Channels for Kit Users

When it comes to customer experience, your job isn't over once the Raspberry Pi kit is sold and shipped; providing a robust support system for your kit users is equally crucial. Consider establishing multiple channels of support to cater to users' varying preferences and technology comfort levels.

Pi Profits

Start by setting up a comprehensive FAQ section on your website addressing common queries about assembly, usage, and troubleshooting. This self-help tool can be a first stop for users facing issues.

In addition, offer live support through email, phone, or web chat. Trained personnel can provide real-time assistance, adding a human touch to tech support. Don't forget about harnessing the power of social media platforms. Quick response time to comments, DMs, or Tweets not only resolves issues but also portrays your brand as customer-centric.

Moreover, consider creating a community forum where users can exchange ideas, solutions, and even share their Raspberry Pi projects. Peer-to-peer interaction can often provide unique solutions and create a sense of belonging among users, leading to long-term brand loyalty.

Remember, in the world of Raspberry Pi, your customer support channels aren't just about solving problems; they're about fostering an engaged, enthusiastic community of makers, learners, and innovators.

Gary Covella, Ph.D.

Marketing Strategies: Online and Offline

In the realm of marketing your Raspberry Pi kits, both online and offline strategies hold equal sway. Embrace the power of digital marketing via social media, SEO, and targeted email campaigns. Social media platforms, especially those that favor visual content, can serve as the perfect stage for demonstrating the capabilities of your Raspberry Pi kits. A well-optimized website with engaging content and clear call-to-actions can attract organic traffic and lead to higher conversions. Meanwhile, personalized email campaigns can nurture relationships with your existing customer base, turning one-time buyers into repeat customers.

At the same time, don't neglect the influence of offline marketing. Participate in tech expos, school and college fairs, and maker community events to showcase your products. Building partnerships with local schools, colleges, and hobby clubs can open avenues for bulk orders and also create opportunities for hands-on workshops. And remember, word-of-mouth advertising is just as impactful today

208.

as it was in the pre-internet era. Strive to create a memorable customer experience that compels your users to become your brand ambassadors, recommending your Raspberry Pi kits to their peers and social circles. In conclusion, a balanced, multi-channel marketing approach can help your Raspberry Pi venture reach its maximum potential audience, paving the way for business growth and success.

Customer Feedback and Iterative Improvement

Harnessing the power of customer feedback is an invaluable strategy in your quest to perfect and popularize your Raspberry Pi kits. The raw, unfiltered opinions and experiences of your customers serve as an effective compass, guiding your product improvements. Regularly engage your users through surveys, social media interactions, or even in-person discussions to gather their inputs. This not only helps you understand their needs better but also demonstrates your commitment to customer satisfaction.

Product development is an iterative process, and your Raspberry Pi kits are no exception. Each version of your kit should be an improvement over the last, addressing customer pain points, enhancing user experience, and perhaps even introducing exciting new features based on your customer suggestions. Remember, your customers are your best critics and advisors. Their feedback is your north star, guiding you towards a product that not only meets market needs, but exceeds customer expectations, securing your place in the burgeoning world of Raspberry Pi entrepreneurship.

Collaborations with Educational Institutions

Partnering with educational institutions can open doors to a wealth of opportunities for advancing your Raspberry Pi venture. Schools, colleges, and universities can be fertile testing grounds for your kits, offering real-world environments to validate product functionality and durability. Furthermore, these institutions harbor curious minds constantly in search of hands-on, practical learning tools — a void your Raspberry Pi kits are perfectly suited to fill.

Pi Profits

Educators are always on a quest for innovative learning aids that can bring abstract concepts to life. Your Raspberry Pi kits, with their versatility and adaptability, can serve as an ideal tool for this purpose. They can be used in teaching a multitude of subjects, from computer science to robotics, from art to agriculture technology. Collaborative projects can be initiated with these institutions, integrating your kits into their curriculum and co-developing lesson plans.

Such collaborations can also help build brand recognition and credibility for your Raspberry Pi kits, especially if the institutions you partner with are renowned in the field of technology and education. These partnerships will not be one-sided, as you'd be contributing to the institutions' mission of providing quality, experiential education, thereby nurturing the next generation of innovators and problem-solvers. With strategic collaborations, the educational sector can serve as a powerful launch pad propelling your Raspberry Pi venture to new heights.

211.

Gary Covella, Ph.D.

Expanding the Range of Kits

While the educational sector offers vast potential, it's important to not overlook other markets ripe for your Raspberry Pi kits. Consider hobbyists and tinkerers, who are often on the lookout for the next fun project. There's a growing community of tech enthusiasts interested in DIY projects — from setting up home automation systems to creating their own gaming consoles. Fine-tuning your kits to cater to this diverse audience could potentially unlock a new revenue stream.

Another potential market lies in the entrepreneurial landscape. Startups, particularly those in the tech sphere, are constantly seeking cost-effective and flexible solutions for prototyping and product development. By offering Raspberry Pi kits tailored for this market, you could facilitate quicker and more efficient product development cycles for these businesses.

Finally, don't discount the potential of the art world. Digital art installations, interactive museum exhibits, and music synthesizers are just a few examples of how your kits could be utilized. Working with artists could not only open up another customer base, but it could also lead to innovative uses of the Raspberry Pi that you haven't even imagined yet.

Remember, the beauty of Raspberry Pi lies in its adaptability. With a little creativity and strategic targeting, the possibilities for your venture are vast and varied.

Monetizing Your Raspberry Pi Venture

Identify Your Target Audience: First, determine who your customer is. This could be educators, hobbyists, tech startups, or artists. Understanding their needs, interests, and challenges is crucial to create and sell Raspberry Pi kits they will value.

Product Creation: Next, develop your Raspberry Pi kits tailored to each audience. For example, a kit for educators might include educational software, while a kit for tech startups might include advanced prototyping tools.

Gary Covella, Ph.D.

Pricing Strategy: After determining the cost to produce each kit, set your pricing. Remember, value-based pricing can often yield higher returns than cost-plus pricing. This means setting a price based on how much your customers believe your product is worth, which could potentially be much more than what it costs to produce.

Marketing and Promotion: Utilize digital marketing strategies to reach your audience. This could be through social media, blogging about interesting Raspberry Pi projects, or partnering with influencers in your target sectors. Make sure to highlight the unique benefits of your kits and how they can solve your customers' challenges.

Sales Channels: Decide where to sell your kits. This could be on your own website, through online retailers like Amazon, or even at local maker fairs and tech conventions.

Partnerships and Collaborations: Consider partnering with educational institutions, tech startups, or artists to showcase what can be achieved with your products. This not only brings in direct sales but also acts as a powerful marketing tool.

214.

Pi Profits

Customer Support and Community Building:
Last but certainly not least, provide
excellent customer service and build a
community around your brand. This could
be through online forums, user groups,
or workshops where customers can share
ideas and provide valuable feedback.
Remember, a happy customer is a repeat
customer, and can often bring in
additional sales through positive word-
of-mouth.

Gary Covella, Ph.D.

216.

CHAPTER 11: BUILDING VPN SERVERS FOR ENHANCED PRIVACY

In this fast-paced world, where the internet is as integral to our lives as air and water, privacy has become a hot-button issue. As we dive into Chapter 11, we're going to explore a solution that's as ingenious as it is effective — leveraging the power of Raspberry Pi to build your very own VPN server. Not only does this provide a robust line of defense against prying eyes on the web, but it also opens up an avenue for a potentially profitable entrepreneurial venture. Whether you're worried about internet snoops, keen on securing your digital footprint, or an entrepreneur seeking a fresh business idea, buckle up! This chapter promises a fulfilling ride into the world of VPN servers and enhanced privacy.

Gary Covella, Ph.D.

The Rising Need for Personal Online Security

In an era where the digital landscape is continuously evolving, personal online security has rapidly transitioned from a luxury to a necessity. Increased reliance on the internet for everyday tasks has catapulted the number of online threats, with cybercriminals becoming more sophisticated in their approach. These threats range from identity theft and phishing to the troubling rise of ransomware attacks. Our personal data, our digital identity, is under constant scrutiny and potential risk. This situation has led to a surge in the demand for robust, personal online security solutions. As we navigate this digital labyrinth, a Virtual Private Network (VPN) emerges as a beacon of hope. A VPN server, especially a self-hosted one, adds a much-needed layer of security to our online presence. It encrypts our data, disguises our online footprint, and gives us the keys to the internet's global city by bypassing geographical restrictions. And the best part? With the right tools and a bit of tech-savviness, we can set up our VPN server, a brilliant solution to safeguard our

218.

digital selves. Let's delve into how Raspberry Pi, a tiny yet potent computer, can be a game-changer in this space.

Basics of Virtual Private Networks (VPNs)

A Virtual Private Network, or VPN, is a secure tunnel between your device and the internet. VPNs protect your online traffic from snooping, interference, and censorship. More importantly, they can mask your IP address, making your online actions virtually untraceable. In essence, VPNs add a security layer to both public and private networks, including broadband and internet hotspots.

With the Raspberry Pi's compact size and powerful capabilities, it serves as an excellent VPN server. Particularly for tech enthusiasts looking to ensure privacy and control over their digital data. By using Raspberry Pi as a VPN server, you have the exclusive control, where you know who has access, thereby enhancing your online security. Moreover, it provides an affordable solution in comparison to subscription-based VPN services. Let's start by understanding what Raspberry Pi is and its functionality in the world of VPN servers.

Configuring Raspberry Pi as a VPN Server

Raspberry Pi, the credit-card-sized powerhouse, is a cost-effective and customizable computer that offers the potential to learn, experiment, and create. It's about as minimal as a computer gets but holds the promise of endless innovation. This mighty munchkin packs in all the functionalities of a traditional computer, including a memory, a processor, and it can even output to a monitor. It runs on Linux, a free operating system, which makes it an attractive option for tech enthusiasts looking for a high degree of customization.

Setting up a Raspberry Pi as a VPN server might sound daunting, but the process is relatively straightforward. First, you need to install a suitable operating system. Many Raspberry Pi users prefer Raspbian, a Debian-based operating system specifically designed for this tiny titan. Then, you'll need to download VPN software. OpenVPN is a popular choice, thanks to its robust security measures and open-source platform. After configuring the necessary settings, you can connect your devices to the VPN, and voila! You've got your private, secure connection to the internet.

This setup can be done in an afternoon and, once completed, offers a secure, private, and reliable internet connection, all hosted by you, and at a fraction of the cost of a commercial VPN service. So, why wait? Let's dive in and transform this little computer into a secure digital fortress.

Understanding and Setting Security Protocols

Though Raspberry Pi is inherently secure, employing additional security protocols is crucial in a world where digital threats are on the rise. Like any computer system, the Raspberry Pi can also become a target for unauthorized access if not properly secured. But don't worry! There are some simple steps you can take to increase the security of your system.

Gary Covella, Ph.D.

The first step is to change the default password that comes with Raspbian. This makes it slightly more difficult for unauthorized users to gain access. Another smart move is to regularly update and upgrade your system. Raspbian provides security patches and system improvements through updates, so regular maintenance is a must. Furthermore, disabling unnecessary network services and setting up a firewall can further secure your Raspberry Pi from unwanted intrusions.

Remember, the goal is to make the system as impervious to outside attacks as possible, so every measure counts. With these precautions in place, you're well on your way to turning your Raspberry Pi into a safe and secure hub of innovation.

Offering Customizable Geolocation Options

Geolocation options provide a unique advantage to your Raspberry Pi, ushering in a whole new world of location-based functionalities. Whether you're looking to create a location-aware device or simply want to spoof your location to access geo-restricted content, the

Raspberry Pi's versatility has you covered. It works by leveraging IP data or integrating with GPS modules, depending on your specific needs and project requirements. This customizable geolocation feature allows you to fine-tune your Raspberry Pi projects, thus offering a level of personalization that amplifies the element of user control. This is another reason why the Raspberry Pi is a darling among tech enthusiasts, educators, and innovators worldwide. Its innate adaptability to cater to such a diverse array of project requirements puts it in a league of its own. But remember, with power comes responsibility; always use these location features ethically and within legal boundaries.

Bandwidth Management and Optimizations

Managing and optimizing bandwidth is a critical aspect of your Raspberry Pi's performance. Efficient bandwidth use ensures that your device runs smoothly, regardless of the number of applications or the level of traffic it handles. There are several techniques you can deploy to optimize bandwidth, such as Quality of Service (QoS) settings, traffic shaping, and even using lighter versions of your favorite applications. Keep in mind that effective bandwidth management isn't just about increasing speed; it's about ensuring stability and reliability in your Raspberry Pi's performance. A well-managed Raspberry Pi not only performs better but also offers a superior user experience, which in turn is likely to lead to more successful and impactful projects. However, always remember that all these optimizations have to be balanced with your project requirements and ethical considerations.

Pricing Strategies for Personal VPN Services

When it comes to pricing strategies for Personal VPN Services using your Raspberry Pi, there is a broad spectrum of possibilities you can consider. Start by examining the costs associated with setting up and maintaining your VPN. This should include the price of the Raspberry Pi itself, any additional hardware necessary, and the cost of your time in terms of setup and maintenance. Once you've established an understanding of your baseline costs, you can start to look at how to price your services.

Pi Profits

One approach is a subscription-based model. This provides a steady stream of income and allows you to forecast future revenues with a greater level of accuracy. You can offer tiered pricing, with different levels providing varying degrees of service, speed, or data usage. Alternatively, you might consider a flat-rate pricing model, where users pay a fixed amount for unlimited access.

Whatever strategy you choose, remember to consider the competitive landscape. What are other VPN services charging? What value do they offer their customers? Can you match or exceed that value while maintaining profitability? Your pricing should reflect the value you provide, yet also be attractive enough to draw in customers.

Whether you're setting this up for personal use or considering a Raspberry Pi VPN as a business venture, your pricing strategy will be crucial in determining its success. But remember, always ensure that your services are offered ethically, within the boundaries of the law, and with the utmost respect for your users' privacy.

Gary Covella, Ph.D.

Marketing in the Age of Digital Privacy

In the era of growing digital privacy concerns, marketing your Raspberry Pi VPN services requires a unique approach. As we enter this new digital age, trust and transparency have become the new currency. It's no longer just about advertising your services; it's about educating the customer, making them aware of the benefits of your services and how you prioritize their privacy.

Use traditional channels like social media advertising, digital marketing, email newsletters, and blogging to reach your potential customers. But, don't just sell. Tell stories that matter to your audience. Show them that you understand their privacy concerns and are there to provide a solution. Highlight the features of your VPN service that ensure safe, secure, and reliable connectivity.

However, remember that in this new age, word-of-mouth and organic recommendations are more influential than ever. Therefore, encourage customer testimonials, share user experiences and keep an open line of communication with

226.

your customer base. A satisfied customer will often be your best marketing tool.

While you're at it, don't forget the power of Search Engine Optimization (SEO). Optimize your website and blog content for search engines to reach a wider audience. Provide high-quality, informational content that educates the visitor, and they'll see you as a trusted authority in the field.

Finally, in this digital age, keeping your customers' trust is paramount. Always respect your users' privacy and operate ethically. Doing so will not only make you stand out but also ensure your venture's longevity and success.

Remember, in the world of digital privacy, trust and transparency aren't just good business practices—they're the foundation of your business.

Customer Support and Troubleshooting

When it comes to customer support and troubleshooting, the golden rule is to never leave your customer in the dark. A fast, efficient, and user-friendly support system not only resolves issues but also fortifies customer trust and loyalty. Employ a multi-channel approach to cover all bases, with email support, FAQs, live chat, and even social media platforms. In fact, a real-time help desk is a fantastic tool to impress your users with your responsiveness.

But remember, it's not just about speed. The quality of support matters just as much, if not more. Your support team must be knowledgeable, courteous, and empathetic to customer concerns. Encourage them to go above and beyond in helping users—because a customer helped is a customer saved. Also, proactive support can work wonders. This means spotting and resolving issues before they affect the user.

As for troubleshooting, it's paramount to have clean, clear, and comprehensive guides available. This empowers users to fix minor issues themselves, saving time and frustration. Similarly, major issues need swift attention and resolution. Regularly update and maintain your tech, and stay transparent with users about any downtime or issues.

And finally, always remember to value feedback. Whether positive or negative, feedback is your secret weapon for improvement. Make it easy for users to share their thoughts and suggestions, and prove that you take their opinion seriously by implementing changes. This transparency and commitment to improvement will foster a strong relationship with your users, and that's what customer support and troubleshooting is all about.

Staying Updated with VPN Protocols and Threats

There's no denying the vitality of staying updated with VPN protocols and threats in this digital age. As the cyber-world evolves, so does its inherent risks, and VPNs are your first line of defense against these lurking dangers. Regularly updating your VPN protocols ensures you're equipped with the latest security features and encryption techniques, fortifying your defense against cyberattacks.

In the same vein, understanding emerging threats is crucial. New vulnerabilities and attack methods are discovered every day. Being aware of these threats allows you to proactively safeguard against them. Adopt a proactive mentality: don't wait for an attack, stay ahead of it.

Gary Covella, Ph.D.

Be it data leakage, weak encryption, or IP leaks, every threat carries the potential to wreak havoc on your online security. By staying educated about these potential pitfalls, you can take steps to mitigate risk and guarantee your online ventures remain secure and thriving.

Remember, knowing your enemy is half the battle won. So learn about potential threats, stay updated on VPN protocols, and ensure your entrepreneurial journey floats in safe waters.

In the words of Benjamin Franklin, "An ounce of prevention is worth a pound of cure." So, get that ounce of prevention by keeping your VPN up-to-date and being vigilant about cybersecurity threats.

Monetizing Your VPN Knowledge

Step 1: Identify and Master your Niche

Start off by identifying a VPN niche that aligns with your interests and expertise. It could be anything from VPN for gaming to VPN for small businesses. Once you've pinpointed your niche,

strive to become the go-to expert in
that field.

Step 2: Create an Informative Blog

Leverage the power of content marketing
by starting a blog where you share your
insights, tips, and recommendations
regarding VPN protocols and threats.
Ensure your content is valuable,
engaging and updated regularly. With
time, your blog could attract a
significant amount of traffic, which you
can monetize.

Step 3: Affiliate Marketing

Join affiliate programs of various VPN
services. With every purchase made
through your affiliate links, you earn a
commission. The key here is to promote
services that you trust and believe in.

Step 4: Offer Consultation Services

Once you've established yourself as a
credible and reliable source of
information, you can offer personalized
consultation services to businesses and
individuals. Help them choose the right
VPN service or assist them in securing
their digital infrastructure.

Gary Covella, Ph.D.

Step 5: Educational Materials

Develop training courses, e-books, or webinars to educate people about the importance of VPNs and how to use them effectively. Platforms like Udemy or Coursera can host your courses, or you can sell them directly from your website.

Step 6: Advertisements

Once your blog or website traffic grows, you can monetize your platform further through ads. Platforms like Google AdSense can be a good starting point.

Remember, authenticity and trust are critical in this game. Always prioritize your audience's needs and provide them with genuine value. This isn't a get-rich-quick scheme, but a journey that requires consistency, dedication, and smart work. So buckle up, and let's make some money!

CHAPTER 12: AGRICULTURAL TECH WITH RASPBERRY PI

Welcome to Chapter 12, where we delve into the fascinating world of Agricultural Tech with Raspberry Pi. A promising frontier in farming, the marriage of technology and agriculture has opened doors to unprecedented efficiency and productivity. But who would've thought that this tiny computer could play such a massive role in this revolution? In this chapter, we're going to explore how the Raspberry Pi can optimize irrigation, enhance crop monitoring, and even automate farming tasks. Whether you're a tech enthusiast looking to venture into agriculture, or a seasoned farmer looking to modernize your operations, this chapter promises insights that could transform your agricultural pursuits into a profitable innovation. So let's dig in, and sow the seeds of technological transformation in your farming practices!

Gary Covella, Ph.D.

The Revolution of Smart Farming

Modern agriculture stands at an exciting crossroads, with traditional farming methods making way for intelligent, tech-driven practices. This shift, often referred to as "smart farming," has been largely facilitated by little marvels of technology such as the Raspberry Pi. This compact computer, no larger than a credit card, has proved to be a game-changer in the agricultural sector.

Deployed in the heart of a lush green field, a Raspberry Pi can gather data about soil moisture, temperature, and light conditions, feeding this information into a system that controls irrigation, fertilizers, and pesticides. It can count the number of fruits on a tree, monitor their ripeness, and even predict yields. This level of automation not only saves time and resources but also enables precise, data-driven decision making.

If you think about it, the Pi in Raspberry Pi could just as well stand for 'Precision farming,' as it brings an unprecedented level of accuracy and efficiency to the field, literally and

234.

figuratively. In the following sections, we'll take a closer look at these applications, providing a step-by-step guide on how you can deploy your Raspberry Pi to create a smart farm. So grab your Raspberry Pi, put on your farmer's hat, and get ready for an exciting journey into the future of farming!

Introduction to Precision Agriculture

Precision agriculture, or precision farming, is the future-focused farming approach on steroids. It's like giving a farmer superhuman abilities to see, understand, and react to every minor detail in the field. Thanks to tiny yet robust computers like Raspberry Pi, these futuristic farming methods are no longer confined to the pages of a science fiction novel, they're becoming the 'new normal.'

The beauty of precision agriculture lies in its detail-oriented methodology. It's not about applying a one-size-fits-all solution - it's about recognizing that each plant, each square foot of soil, has its unique needs. With Raspberry Pi and a handful of sensors, farmers can

235.

examine each plant individually, even down to the leaf level, and cater to its specific requirements.

From identifying diseases before they spread to optimizing water and fertilizer usage based on plant needs, precision agriculture aims to reduce waste, increase yields, and ultimately boost profitability.

The following chapters will guide you through setting up your Raspberry Pi for precision farming, from programming the device to choosing sensors to understanding the data. This journey might mark the birth of a new era in your agricultural endeavors, one where you're not just working on the land but with the land. So, let's dive in!

Monitoring Soil Moisture and Weather Conditions

Understanding the moisture levels in the soil and the weather conditions are pivotal aspects of precision agriculture. The Raspberry Pi, armed with a few sensors, becomes a vigilant guardian, faithfully monitoring these critical parameters. Soil moisture sensors, integrated with the Raspberry

Pi, help farmers understand the thirst of their plants, allowing them to irrigate optimally. Overwatering or underwatering can harm the crops, but with accurate moisture data, farmers can maintain the perfect balance.

Weather conditions, too, significantly influence the health and growth of crops. Here's where a weather station kit for Raspberry Pi comes into play. It tracks parameters like temperature, humidity, barometric pressure, and rainfall, all of which are crucial for informed decision-making in farming. With real-time weather data, farmers can respond swiftly to changing conditions, protecting their crops from unexpected weather events. Up next, we'll delve into how to set up these monitoring mechanisms using the Raspberry Pi. Set sail on this journey of precision agriculture, and let the Raspberry Pi be your compass.

Automated Irrigation Systems

No more guessing, no more depending on unreliable weather forecasts. With the help of Raspberry Pi, you can create an automated irrigation system, tailored to your crop's specific needs. This system, powered by precise data from your soil moisture and weather sensors, can control your irrigation schedule and volume down to the last drop. Imagine a setup where the sprinklers kick into action when the soil gets too dry or turn off when it's about to rain! You're not only saving water but also ensuring each plant gets the right amount of moisture it needs.

Setting up the automated irrigation system is an easy-peasy task. You'll need a relay module to control the water pump or solenoid valve, a moisture sensor to detect the soil's moisture level, and of course, a Raspberry Pi to be the brain of the operation. You'll wire them together, install the necessary software on your Pi, and voila! Your automated and eco-friendly irrigation system is ready to roll.

The next chapter will guide you through every step of setting this up, including the wiring diagram and the coding part. But don't worry, even if you're new to this, we've got you covered. It's time to bring in a technological revolution to your farm, one Raspberry Pi at a time. So buckle up, and let's get irrigating!

238.

Integrating Cameras for Livestock Monitoring

Farm animals are not just sources of income, they're part of your extended family. Just like you wouldn't leave your children unattended, why should your livestock be any different? With Raspberry Pi, you can create a reliable, cost-effective livestock monitoring system that keeps an eye on your animals 24/7. This nifty setup uses a network of cameras to monitor their movement, eating habits, and general health. Unexpected behavior? You'll be the first to know. Not around? No problem. You can access the live feed on your smartphone or PC, wherever you are.

Setting up your camera network is no more challenging than setting up the irrigation system. You'll need a Pi camera or a USB webcam, a Raspberry Pi (of course), and some open-source software. We'll guide you through the process, from installing the camera to writing the code that makes everything work together. It's like your personal CCTV system, customized for your farm.

With this system, you can ensure your livestock are safe, healthy, and thriving, even when you're not physically present. So, are you ready to step up your farming game and secure the well-being of your livestock? Let's dive into the next chapter, where we'll start building your livestock monitoring system, one Raspberry Pi at a time.

Data Analysis for Improved Crop Yields

Just when you thought you had seen it all, Raspberry Pi is about to change your farming game with data analysis. Don't let the term scare you, it's simpler than you think! Basically, we're talking about using Raspberry Pi to collect and analyze data related to your crops and environment. This can include anything from soil pH levels and moisture content to temperature and sunlight exposure.

Sounds complicated? Well, it's not! This minuscule yet mighty marvel uses sensors to collect all this data, which you can then analyze on your computer. Fancy stuff like predicting weather patterns or optimal watering schedules? It's all possible with the power of data analysis.

Remember, the goal here is to optimize your crop yields and reduce waste, and with a Raspberry Pi, even the sky isn't the limit. In the following sections, we'll break down how you can implement this in your farm, step by step, sensor by sensor. So, ready to bring the power of 21st-century data analysis to your farm? Let's swing into action!

Challenges in Implementing Agri-tech Solutions

Sure, integrating technology, especially something as groundbreaking as Raspberry Pi into your farming operations, may seem daunting at first. You might encounter a few bumps in the road — hardware issues, software glitches, or data analysis dilemmas. Heck, you may even find yourself wondering, "Why did I sign up for this in the first place?" But trust me, every bit of sweat is going to be worth it.

There's a learning curve, indeed. But remember, every new venture comes with its own set of challenges. Don't let a few initial hiccups discourage you. Besides, this guide is here to walk you through every step and every snag. Together, we'll troubleshoot, learn, and master the art of utilizing Raspberry Pi in agri-tech. So tighten your seatbelts, folks! The journey might be a tad bumpy, but the destination? A high-tech, highly profitable farm of the future. Let's get the ball rolling, shall we?

Collaborating with Farmers and Agronomists

Working closely with farmers and agronomists is a crucial step towards successful implementation of Raspberry Pi in agri-tech. Why, you ask? Because these are the folks who understand the lay of the land – literally! They know the soil, the climate, and the crops better than anyone else. It's their years of experience and in-depth knowledge that can help tailor the technology to the unique needs of your farm.

Farmers can provide valuable insights into the practical aspects of farming, while agronomists can bridge the gap between traditional farming methods and the latest technological advancements. Collaborating with them involves understanding their daily challenges, their needs, and their goals.

Pi Profits

Remember, the ultimate aim of introducing Raspberry Pi into the farming world isn't just about planting a flag in the future. It's about cultivating a profitable and sustainable present. So, roll up your sleeves, get your hands dirty, and dive into the world of farming. After all, the best way to predict the future of farming is to invent it. Let's take this leap together, and believe me, the profits will follow.

Economic Benefits and ROI for Farmers

Implementing Raspberry Pi in agri-tech isn't just an exciting merger of tech and tradition, it's a bankable investment promising an appealing Return on Investment (ROI) for farmers. By automating mundane tasks and precision monitoring of crop health, the Raspberry Pi proves its weight in gold. It cuts down manual labor, optimizes resource usage, and reduces waste — all of which translate into cost-savings.

Moreover, farmers leveraging this potent micro-computer can maximize yield quality and quantity, leading to a boost in income. The economic benefits don't

Gary Covella, Ph.D.

stop here — the technological edge can also make farms eligible for various tech grants and incentives, further sweetening the deal. So, Raspberry Pi isn't just a ticket to join the high-tech band, it's your golden ticket to a lucrative future.

The Future of Agriculture with Raspberry Pi

The Raspberry Pi in agriculture is not merely a passing trend, but rather a glimpse into the future of farming. Imagine a world where the art of agriculture meets the precision of technology, where every plant has a bespoke care plan, and every crop is nurtured to perfection. This is no longer a pipe dream but a reality within our grasp, thanks to the Raspberry Pi.

Using sensors and data analytics, the Raspberry Pi can monitor and analyze numerous variables that directly affect crop health, such as soil moisture, temperature, and nutrient levels. This data-driven approach results in improved crop health, early detection and mitigation of potential issues, thereby ensuring a more abundant and healthier crop yield.

Pi Profits

Furthermore, the Raspberry Pi opens the door to innovative applications such as automated irrigation systems, drone crop monitoring, and even predictive analytics to forecast crop diseases. These advancements not only make farming more efficient but also more sustainable by optimizing resource usage and minimizing waste.

But beyond the fields, Raspberry Pi is fostering a new generation of tech-savvy farmers. By equipping them with the tools and knowledge to leverage technology, we're cultivating a future where tech and farming go hand in hand, driving profitability and sustainability. In this future, every farm will be a smart farm, and every farmer, a tech pioneer. So, let's embark on this exciting journey together, and remember, the future of farming is not just to live in but to create and the tool to do that is in your hands - the Raspberry Pi.

Here's how you turn this pocket-sized powerhouse into a money-making machine.

Start small and grow smart: Begin by automating a small garden or greenhouse. Use Raspberry Pi to monitor and manage parameters like water, light, and

245.

temperature levels. As your system gets more sophisticated, expand to larger plots.

Sell your smart farming solutions: Present your success to local farmers and convince them about the efficiency of your automated system. Sell them your Raspberry Pi-powered solutions or offer it as a service, maintaining and upgrading their farming systems.

Educate others: Host workshops for farming communities, schools, or local clubs. Teach them the ins and outs of using Raspberry Pi for agriculture and charge a fee for your expertise.

Create a niche blog or YouTube channel: Share your journey and learnings online. Monetize through advertisements, sponsored content, or by selling your own guidebooks and tutorials.

Develop and sell custom software: As you gain more experience, you can develop custom farm management software that works with Raspberry Pi. This software could be sold to agricultural businesses around the globe.

Remember folks, this little device might be small but it has enormous potential.

Pi Profits

It's not just about making money, but about making a difference. So get out there and show the world what a farmer with a Raspberry Pi can do!

Gary Covella, Ph.D.

248.

CHAPTER 13: PI-BASED ROBOTICS AND DRONES

Welcome to Chapter 13, where we're going to dive into the buzzing world of Pi-based Robotics and Drones! Just imagine, in your hands, you've got the power to create intelligent machines and high-flying gadgets that are not only super fun but can also attract serious cash. From automated vacuum cleaners that keep your floors spotless, to high-tech drones that can capture stunning aerial photos or deliver pizza right to your backyard. The possibilities are as limitless as your imagination. Just as we've seen with a simple garden, once you master the principles and get a taste of what Raspberry Pi can do, you'll see opportunities everywhere. So let's buckle up and discover how this tiny tech dynamo can turn you into a robotics entrepreneur!

Gary Covella, Ph.D.

Introduction to Robotics with Raspberry Pi

The Raspberry Pi, despite its compact size, is a powerhouse for robotics. This tiny computer's extraordinary versatility opens the doors to a myriad of robotic applications. Robotics isn't just assembling motors and gears anymore; it's about embedding intelligence into your creations. With the Raspberry Pi at your disposal, you can breathe life into your robots, from autonomous cars whizzing around your living room to expressive robots that interact with people.

You might be asking, "Why Raspberry Pi for robotics?" The answer is simple: flexibility, affordability, and a vibrant community support. By using the Raspberry Pi for your robotic projects, you can leverage the power of open-source software and a vast repository of community knowledge. Additionally, with a variety of available sensors and modules compatible with the Raspberry Pi, the sky's the limit when it comes to the functionality you can build into your robots.

So whether you're a hobbyist looking to dabble in robotics, an entrepreneur eyeing the next big robotic application, or a curious learner wanting to step into the captivating world of robotics, Raspberry Pi is your perfect launchpad. Together, let's embark on this exciting journey and uncover the genius of Raspberry Pi in the realm of robotics.

Understanding Motors, Sensors, and Actuators

Before we dive into crafting mechanical marvels with Raspberry Pi, let's acquaint ourselves with the basic building blocks of robotics — motors, sensors and actuators. These components are the nerve, brain, and muscles of any robot, driving its movements, perceiving its environment, and executing actions respectively.

Motors, in the world of robotics, are akin to what hearts are to humans — they keep the system going by converting electrical energy into motion. Depending on your project requirements, you might opt for DC motors, servo motors, or stepper motors, each with its own unique characteristics and advantages.

Sensors, on the other hand, provide your robot with a semblance of perception, allowing it to interact intelligently with its environment. From ultrasonic sensors for measuring distance to temperature sensors for detecting heat, there's a sensor for almost every application you can dream of.

Actuators are the real action heroes here. They translate the robot's decision into physical action, making your robot do its intended job. This could involve rotating a camera, lifting an arm, or even propelling a drone into the sky.

Building a Raspberry Pi-Controlled Robot

Now that we've laid down the groundwork, let's move onto the crux of the matter – building your first Raspberry Pi-controlled robot. Imagine having a personal assistant that performs tasks at your command, a tiny bot that brings your morning coffee, or an automated vacuum cleaner that keeps your floor spotless. Doesn't it sound like a dream come true?

Pi Profits

Building your robot involves a mix of hardware assembly and software programming. You'll start by selecting the right chassis for your bot. It's the skeletal structure that houses all the internal components like motors, Raspberry Pi, sensors, and power supply. Depending on your project requirements and design preferences, you could choose from a variety of chassis options available in the market, ranging from simple two-wheeled designs to complex multi-legged ones.

Next, you'll connect the motors, sensors and actuators to your Raspberry Pi. The beauty of Raspberry Pi lies in its versatile GPIO (General Purpose Input/Output) pins that allow you to interface with a variety of hardware. Remember to pay careful attention to the wiring - a wrong connection could potentially damage your components.

Once your hardware is all set up, it's time to breathe life into your robot with some code. You'll be using Python - a powerful and easy-to-learn programming language that has in-built libraries for controlling motors and interfacing with sensors. With a few lines of code, you

Gary Covella, Ph.D.

can make your robot move, react to its environment, and perform tasks.

And there you have it, your personal Raspberry Pi-controlled robot! But remember, this is just the beginning. The world of robotics is vast and ever-evolving. Keep experimenting, keep learning, and keep innovating. Who knows, your next invention could change the world!

Drones: Aerial Photography and More

Now, let's soar into the world of drones. Imagine capturing breathtaking aerial footage, or delivering parcels to doorsteps with a touch of a button. With Raspberry Pi, such dreams can swiftly morph into reality. At the heart of your drone is the flight controller, a mini computer that interprets your commands and adjusts the drone's motors to achieve the desired flight path. The Raspberry Pi, with its compact size and powerful processing capabilities, serves as an excellent flight controller.

But that's not all, my friends! With the addition of a Pi camera, your drone can capture high-quality photos and videos, opening up possibilities for aerial photography, surveillance, and environmental monitoring. The flexible GPIO pins of the Raspberry Pi allow you to add more functionality to your drone – how about a temperature sensor for atmospheric studies, or a claw for aerial deliveries?

As with any Raspberry Pi project, programming is a crucial part of building your drone. Python's simplicity and power come to the rescue again, enabling you to control your drone with a few lines of code. However, flying a drone also involves understanding some basic principles of aerodynamics. But don't fret, the learning curve is part of the fun.

The sky's the limit when it comes to drone applications, and with a Raspberry Pi in your toolkit, the journey is bound to be exciting.

Navigational Algorithms and Object Avoidance

When it comes to navigational algorithms and object avoidance, Raspberry Pi really flexes its tech muscles. Like a seasoned navigator, it charts the course for drones, ensuring a safe and smooth journey from point A to point B. Integrating a Raspberry Pi with sensors like ultrasonic or infrared opens up a world of possibilities for real-time object detection and avoidance. This isn't just about preventing collisions—it's about crafting smart, responsive drones that can adapt to their environments on the fly.

Think of it like this: you're teaching your drone to see and understand its surroundings, making split-second decisions to dodge obstacles. And the best part? It's all done through Python, a language known for its readability and efficiency. You'll be using libraries like OpenCV for image processing, and PID control loops for precise maneuvering.

Sure, it might seem daunting at first, but as you dive deeper into the world of navigational algorithms and object avoidance, you'll find it incredibly rewarding. Remember, every line of code you write brings your drone one step closer to becoming a fully autonomous flying machine. So, let's gear up, put on our coding hats, and make our

Raspberry Pi drones not just fly, but soar!

Remote Control and Real-time Feedback

Controlling drones remotely coupled with real-time feedback is a facet that separates the wheat from the chaff in the drone tech landscape. With Raspberry Pi, this dream becomes a reality. Imagine you're miles away, comfortably perched in your armchair yet in full command of your drone soaring in the sky. Raspberry Pi makes it possible. It facilitates real-time feedback, sending crucial data about speed, altitude, and GPS coordinates right to your fingertips.

The magic sauce? A concoction of Python along with various open source libraries. From live-streaming video footage to receiving sensor data, you command every aspect. As you tinker and experiment, you'll realize the power you wield and the possibilities that arise. The process might feel like taming a wild stallion initially. However, once you get the hang of it, you'll have a drone that doesn't just respond to commands, but provides valuable insights and data. This is no toy; it's a tool, an extension of your will, reaching places you can't, seeing things you can't, and doing things you wouldn't have imagined.

So, buckle up, future drone masters! With Raspberry Pi and your unyielding spirit, we're about to embark on a journey that'll redefine boundaries and tear up preconceived notions, one line of code at a time. Let's not just rule the skies, let's redefine them.

Challenges in Flight and Motion

While the possibilities with Raspberry Pi are virtually limitless, conquering flight and motion is not without its share of challenges. The laws of aerodynamics aren't easily bent to the will of code. Unpredictable wind patterns, altitude fluctuation, and maintaining balance are just a few hurdles on the path to airborne supremacy. In the world of digital code, these are real, tangible problems demanding solutions. But don't let the turbulence dismay you. With each line of code, each failed test flight, you're not just debugging, you're evolving, adapting, overcoming. You're bridging the gap between the binary and the physical, transforming a hunk of metal into a dynamic, responsive entity. You're not just writing code; you're crafting a symphony of movement, a ballet of flight. So, let's dive in! Let's dissect these challenges, unravel the mysteries of flight, and hone our craft until the sky isn't a limit, but a canvas for our creations.

Expanding Capabilities with AI

Raspberry Pi isn't just about mastering the mechanics; it's about embracing the future. And the future, my friends, is Artificial Intelligence. This isn't some gimmicky science fiction trope. No, siree! AI is here, now, weaving its way into every aspect of our lives, amplifying our abilities, and augmenting our reality. With AI, your Raspberry Pi drone isn't just a machine; it becomes an extension of you, learning from you, adapting to you. It becomes a partner, a collaborator, an accomplice in your airborne endeavors. AI can help analyze wind conditions, predict weather patterns, optimize flight paths, and so much more. And the best part? You don't need a doctorate in quantum physics to harness the power of AI. With a little patience, a pinch of perseverance, and a healthy dose of curiosity, anyone can inject a bit of intelligence into their Raspberry Pi. So, what are you waiting for? Let's take the leap into the future together, shall we? In the following chapters, we'll explore the basics of AI, tackle some popular algorithms, and teach our drones to think for themselves. After all, the future is only as far away as the next line of code.

Navigating the Bumps on the Road

But hold on to your horses! We're going to hit some bumps on this road. Yes, the path of innovation is not always sunlit and smooth. There will be moments of frustration, times when your drone stubbornly refuses to lift off, or your code sprouts inexplicable errors. But that's part of the game, part of the journey. Remember, every great inventor, every groundbreaking programmer, has faced their fair share of problems. And they've not just survived, they've thrived, transforming each stumbling block into a stepping-stone. This chapter is designed to help you do just that. We're going to explore the most common issues you might encounter on your Raspberry Pi journey. We'll help you diagnose problems, troubleshoot errors, and find solutions. And through it all, we aim to instill in you the most important skill a pioneer can have: resilience. So, buckle up, grit your teeth, and get ready to overcome the hurdles. Because every problem is nothing more than an opportunity in disguise. Let's crack those issues wide open and march on, one line of code at a time.

Engaging in Robotics and Drone Competitions

Diving into the world of Robotics and Drone Competitions is not just about flaunting your tech-savviness. It's about tasting the thrill of competition, rising to the challenge of creating something extraordinary, and showcasing your innovative prowess. These contests provide a platform for your Raspberry Pi-driven drones to shine — a place where you can pit your coding skills against the best in the business, and learn a thing or two in the process. Remember, victory isn't just standing on the podium with a shiny trophy; it's about the journey, the friendships forged, the knowledge gained, and the skills honed. So, how about we strap in, roll up our sleeves, and delve into the electrifying world of robotics and drone competitions? Here, we'll discuss the various types of competitions, the rules of the game, and strategies to ensure you and your drone stand tall amongst the competition. Ladies and gentlemen, start your engines, because we're lifting off into an adventure of a lifetime.

Profiting from your Raspberry Pi Mastery and Robotics Competitions

First, start by mastering your craft. Sink your teeth into learning all about Raspberry Pi, robotics, and drones. Remember, knowledge is power, and in this case, it's potential dollars too.

Second, participate in robotics and drone competitions. This isn't just a test of your skills, but it's also a fantastic opportunity to make connections, gain exposure, and even capture the attention of potential investors or employers.

Pi Profits

Third, consider offering workshops or tutoring sessions for those looking to break into the world of Raspberry Pi and robotics. There's always a demand for skilled teachers in this field, and it's a great way to share your passion while making a buck or two.

Fourth, think about developing your own Raspberry Pi driven products. This could be anything from a clever home automation device to an educational tool for schools. If you've got a unique, marketable idea, then why not take it to the marketplace?

And finally, consider writing about your experiences and knowledge. Whether it's in the form of a blog, an ebook, or even a YouTube channel, sharing your insights can not only bolster your reputation in the industry but also potentially generate ad revenue.

Remember, the world of Raspberry Pi and robotics is vast and versatile, and there's plenty of room for profitability. So, keep your eyes open, your brain buzzing, and your passion for technology burning bright. Who knows where this Raspberry Pi journey will take you?

Gary Covella, Ph.D.

264.

CHAPTER 14: MIRRORING THE FUTURE: SMART MIRRORS

Alright, my friend, buckle up because we're about to dive headfirst into the future. Chapter 14 is all about the magic of smart mirrors. Now, you might be wondering, "what on earth is a smart mirror?" Well, let me enlighten you. Imagine waking up in the morning, walking over to your mirror to check your hair, and instead of just your reflection, you also get to see the day's weather, your calendar, and perhaps even your morning news briefing. Sounds like something out of a sci-fi movie, right? But with Raspberry Pi, this future is within our grasp. So let's get cracking and see how you can build your own smart mirror and maybe even turn it into a profitable venture.

Gary Covella, Ph.D.

The Allure of Futuristic Home Gadgets

Modern consumers are in an incessant pursuit of convenience and efficiency. This chase has ushered in a new age of home gadgets that surpass the ordinary and tread into the terrain of the extraordinary. At the forefront of this revolution is the 'Smart Mirror,' an intriguing fusion of design, technology, and functionality. Boasting a myriad of useful features, a smart mirror can display everything from weather forecasts and traffic reports to personal health data and social media notifications, all while you're doing your morning routine. This captivating gadget has the power to transform mundane tasks into a holistic and seamless experience, effectively reinventing our perception of household objects. The allure of such futuristic home gadgets lies in their ability to weave technology into the fabric of everyday life, making information access mere child's play and enhancing lifestyle quality. With Raspberry Pi at its core, creating such an innovative product is no longer a distant dream but a tangible reality you can profit from.

266.

The Raspberry Pi: Breathing Life into Your Smart Mirror

Your journey into the realm of Smart Mirrors begins with the heart of the operation: the Raspberry Pi. This small yet mighty computer board is the perfect tool to power your innovative contraption. With its cost-effective price point and versatile functionality, the Raspberry Pi makes technology democratization a reality. It's no longer just the big tech companies that can afford to create smart devices – now, anyone with a bit of creativity and a willingness to learn can join the game.

The Raspberry Pi operates on a Linux-based operating system, making it a playground for software enthusiasts. This compact computer offers a plethora of connectivity options, including USB, Ethernet, and HDMI, simplifying the integration with other hardware components of your Smart Mirror. Not to mention its wireless capabilities which make accessing the internet a breeze.

Now, the question you might be asking yourself is "How do I go from a Raspberry Pi to a Smart Mirror?" Well, the basic principle revolves around setting up the Raspberry Pi to run a web page in full-screen mode, which is then displayed on a monitor placed behind a two-way mirror. It's a simple yet ingenious trick that turns a basic household item into a futuristic gadget. So, are you ready to venture down this rabbit hole and transform your entrepreneurial dreams into a profitable reality? Let's get down to the nitty-gritty of building your very own Smart Mirror with Raspberry Pi.

Incorporating Raspberry Pi and Display Tech

The beauty of Raspberry Pi lies in its modularity and flexibility. At the heart of your Smart Mirror will be a screen, most likely an LCD monitor, connected to your Raspberry Pi. This screen serves as the canvas for your mirrored interface, displaying time, notifications, news, weather forecast, or even your daily workout routine. When selecting a monitor, you'll want to consider factors such as size, resolution, and power consumption. Ideally, you should opt for a monitor with an HDMI interface for seamless integration with the Raspberry Pi.

Pi Profits

Remember, the Raspberry Pi is a jack-of-all-trades and that's what makes it such an instrumental tool. You can program it to display whatever you fancy on your Smart Mirror, from a daily quote to motivate you in the morning to your favorite productivity apps. The only limiting factor is your imagination. Harness the power of this tiny titan to create a Smart Mirror that truly reflects your needs and aspirations.

Integrating APIs: Weather, Calendar, News

APIs, or Application Programming Interfaces, are going to be your best friends when it comes to making your Smart Mirror, well, smart. These programming protocols and tools allow you to fetch real-time data from various sources and bring them right to your mirror. Ever wondered how you could get your mirror to tell you if you need an umbrella before stepping out? Or how you could stay on top of your day's schedule while brushing your teeth? The answer lies in integrating APIs into your Raspberry Pi setup.

For instance, you could use a Weather API to fetch the local weather forecast and display it on your mirror. Calendar APIs can help you sync your schedule and reminders, ensuring you never miss a beat. And how about staying updated with the latest headlines while you get ready for the day? News APIs have got you covered.

All it takes is a bit of coding nitty-gritty, and voila, your mirror transforms into your personal assistant. But don't let the coding part intimidate you. You don't need to be a tech whizz to pull this off. There are plenty of resources and libraries available that make the process of integrating APIs as easy as pie. So, if you're ready to make your mirror a bit more magical, let's dive into the world of APIs.

Voice and Gesture Controls

Who wouldn't want to control their Smart Mirror with just their voice or a wave of their hand? This is where the true genius of your Raspberry Pi comes into play. Integrating voice and gesture controls can make your Smart Mirror not just smart, but intuitively responsive.

Imagine this: you're getting ready in the morning, your hands are busy, but you want to know the traffic situation or change the song playing in the background. With a simple voice command or a predetermined hand gesture, your Smart Mirror obeys. It feels like magic, doesn't it?

Voice controls can be achieved by integrating your Smart Mirror with AI assistants like Google Assistant or Amazon's Alexa. Gesture controls, on the other hand, are a little more high-tech, possibly requiring additional hardware like motion sensors or infrared cameras.

But don't worry, even with these advanced features, the Raspberry Pi makes it a breeze to implement. All you need is a bit of imagination, a touch of creativity, and a willingness to experiment. So let's give your Smart Mirror a dash of Harry Potter and make it come alive!

Design Aesthetics and Customization Options

Your Smart Mirror isn't just a functional gadget, it's a piece of your home decor. And as such, it should mirror (pun intended) your personal style and aesthetic preferences. With the Raspberry Pi, customization is king.

Gary Covella, Ph.D.

From the frame to the interface, every aspect of your Smart Mirror can be designed to suit your taste.

Fancy a vintage wooden frame to complement your rustic home interior? Or perhaps a sleek metallic frame for that modern minimalist look? Your options are only limited by your imagination. But the customization doesn't stop there.

The interface of your Smart Mirror can also be modified to your liking. Want the weather forecast in the top right corner? Or maybe your daily schedule needs to be the first thing you see? You decide.

Add in personalized widgets like your favorite inspirational quotes or daily fun facts. Make your Smart Mirror truly yours.

Remember, the Raspberry Pi is your playground. So go ahead, play around, experiment, and create a Smart Mirror that's uniquely you. After all, who said home automation couldn't be stylish?

Troubleshooting and Optimizations

When you're dealing with technology, especially when it's a DIY project, you're bound to hit a few roadblocks. But don't worry, that's part of the fun! In this section, we'll delve into some common hiccups you might face with your Raspberry Pi-powered Smart Mirror and how to overcome them.

First off, if your display isn't showing up correctly, check your connections. Make sure everything is plugged in where it should be. If that doesn't do the trick, take a look at your coding. A single character can throw everything off!

And what about speed? If your Smart Mirror feels sluggish, there are several optimizations you can do. Consider overclocking your Raspberry Pi (but be careful not to overheat it), or utilizing a lighter Operating System.

But remember, the Raspberry Pi community is HUGE. If you're stuck or need some inspiration, countless forums, guides, and tutorials are just a google search away, ready to lend a hand. So dive in,

273.

don't be afraid to get your hands dirty, and start exploring the amazing world of Raspberry Pi.

Packaging and Shipping Challenges

Shipping your Raspberry Pi creations can be both an exciting and tense endeavor. Even though your project has passed all the troubleshooting stages, shipping and handling pose a new set of challenges. For starters, you'll need to carefully package your product to ensure it survives the journey. Consider using high-quality packaging materials have shock-absorbing properties to protect your device from any potential damage.

Moreover, it's crucial to account for the diverse shipping regulations that vary from one region to another, especially for international shipping. These might relate to battery safety, tech specifications, or import taxes, so be sure to conduct comprehensive research to ensure a smooth delivery.

Keep in mind, your Raspberry Pi projects are more than just products. They are the physical manifestation of your creativity, innovation, and countless hours of hard work. So, when it comes to packaging and shipping, it's worth taking the extra measures to ensure your ingenious inventions reach their new home safe and sound. Remember, a pleased customer could mean a repeat customer, and in the world of Raspberry Pi, word-of-mouth can be your most powerful marketing tool. So, buckle up, do your homework, and get ready to send your Raspberry Pi creations out into the world.

Marketing and Target Audience Analysis

Now let's talk about the bread and butter of any venture - Marketing and Target Audience Analysis. Remember, no matter how groundbreaking your Raspberry Pi creation is, it won't amount to a hill of beans unless it reaches the right people. Your target audience should be at the center of every decision you make, from the design stage right through to shipping.

Start by considering who would benefit the most from your product. Are they tech-savvy gamers looking for the next best console? Or perhaps they're educators seeking interactive teaching tools? Once you've zeroed in on your audience, dig a little deeper. Understand their needs, their desires, their habits. What social media platforms do they frequent? What's their average budget for tech gadgets? This kind of knowledge can be invaluable in shaping your marketing strategy.

Next, carve your unique position in the market. With a product as versatile as Raspberry Pi, it's easy to get lost in the crowd. Promote what sets your creation apart, whether it's the innovative design, the cost-effectiveness, or the unparalleled user experience.

Finally, don't forget to use your satisfied customers as brand ambassadors. Encourage them to spread the word about your fantastic product. After all, there's no better advertising than a happy customer singing your praises. So go ahead, my friend. Dive into the world of marketing and audience analysis. The success of your Raspberry Pi venture depends on it.

Post-Sales Support and Updates

Now that we've nailed down our marketing and audience analysis, let's shift our focus to an equally crucial aspect of your venture – post-sales support and updates. The journey with your customer doesn't end once they've purchased your Raspberry Pi creation. In fact, that's just the beginning.

Offering top-notch post-sales support can be the difference between a one-time purchase and a loyal customer. Make it easy for your customers to reach you. Provide clear instructions for assembly, installation, and troubleshooting, right from the get-go. Regularly check in with them to ensure they're getting the most out of your product. Remember, a happy customer is a repeat customer, and they're more likely to recommend your product to others.

Additionally, keep your product up-to-date with the latest advancements in Raspberry Pi technology. Regular updates not only improve the performance and longevity of your product but also show your customers that you're committed to providing them with the best possible experience.

In a nutshell, post-sales support and updates are the secret ingredients to maintaining a thriving customer base and ensuring the longevity of your venture. So, don't skimp on them!

CHAPTER 15: SHARING KNOWLEDGE: TUTORIALS AND CONTENT CREATION

Welcome to Chapter 15, my friend, where you'll master the art of 'Sharing Knowledge: Tutorials and Content Creation'. Now, you may be wondering why a tech guide is shifting gears to talk about content creation. The answer is simple — education is the most powerful tool you can use to grow your Raspberry Pi venture. As you step into the world of tutorials and content creation, you'll not only empower your audience with knowledge but also establish your authority in the Raspberry Pi space. From creating how-to guides to hosting webinars, you'll learn how to leverage content to connect with your customers, inspire innovation, and drive business growth. So, let's embark on this exciting journey and unlock new avenues for your venture. Remember, when you teach, you learn. So, buckle up and prepare to learn as much as you teach.

Gary Covella, Ph.D.

The Rise of DIY Culture and the Role of Online Tutorials

The Do-It-Yourself (DIY) culture is experiencing an extraordinary boom, largely driven by the quest for knowledge and the satisfaction of creating something hands-on. This surge in interest has carved a niche for online tutorials, playing a crucial role as the main catalyst for people embarking on their DIY journey. In the context of Raspberry Pi, the DIY culture has been nothing short of a revelation. Online tutorials, whether in the form of blog posts, YouTube videos, or detailed instruction guides, have become a valuable resource for enthusiasts to learn, experiment, and innovate. These tutorials eliminate the barriers of technical jargon, providing step-by-step, easy-to-understand information that makes Raspberry Pi accessible to everyone, from a beginner to a seasoned techie. So, in an age where information is at our fingertips, sharing knowledge through online tutorials is the engine that's fueling the DIY culture, fostering a community of creators, innovators, and life-long learners.

Choosing Your Content Medium: Blog, Video, Podcast

The choice of your content medium largely depends on your target audience and the nature of the subject matter. Each medium - be it a blog, video, or podcast - comes with its own unique advantages. Blogs are a firm favorite among those who prefer reading at their own pace and value the ability to refer back to written instructions. This format is also great for SEO purposes, helping you attract organic traffic to your website. Videos, on the other hand, cater to those who are visual learners. They appreciate the ability to see the process in action, especially in the context of Raspberry Pi projects that often involve hands-on work. Then there are podcasts - a rapidly growing medium that capitalizes on the convenience of audio content. Ideal for audiences who prefer to learn on the move, podcasts enable you to dive deep into topics and discussions about Raspberry Pi technology. The key here is to know your audience and their preferences, and to deliver high-quality content that caters to their learning style. Remember, consistency and value delivery should be the cornerstone of your content strategy, regardless of the medium you choose.

Designing a Content Calendar

After selecting your content medium, the next crucial step is designing a content calendar. A well-planned content calendar serves as your roadmap, guiding you through a consistent content creation process. It helps you plan your topics in advance, making sure you cover a broad spectrum of Raspberry Pi applications that cater to different segments of your audience. For instance, one week you might focus on a Raspberry Pi project for beginners, such as setting up a retro gaming console. The next, you could delve into more complex topics for seasoned techies, like building a home automation system. Remember, the key is to keep the content diverse yet relevant. As you fill your content calendar, keep in mind seasonal trends and upcoming events that might interest your audience. Perhaps there's a Raspberry Pi conference, or maybe a new accessory or update is due to be launched — these are perfect opportunities to align your content. Lastly, always allocate time for brainstorming and content production to ensure you maintain a steady stream of quality content.

Crafting Engaging and Comprehensive Raspberry Pi Tutorials

Your Raspberry Pi tutorials should be a mix of engaging narratives and detailed, step-by-step processes designed to help your audience effectively navigate their Raspberry Pi projects. To ensure that your tutorials cater to everyone, vary your content in terms of complexity. Create beginner-friendly tutorials that explain basic concepts and offer simple projects for practice. At the same time, include advanced tutorials for seasoned Raspberry Pi users that delve into more complex projects and concepts. Utilize images, diagrams, and videos where possible to supplement written instructions and provide clearer guidance. Keep the language simple, concise, and jargon-free to ensure comprehension for beginners. Finally, encourage interaction and engagement by including challenges or projects at the end of each tutorial and inviting readers to share their experiences and results. This can foster a sense of community among your readers and make learning more enjoyable and rewarding.

Promoting Content on Social Media

Social media provides a powerful platform to promote your Raspberry Pi content and reach a global audience. Utilize various social media channels, each targeting a different demographic, to share snippets of your tutorials, interesting project ideas, and success stories from your community. For visually appealing content, consider Instagram and Pinterest, where you can post pictures or short videos of your projects. Meanwhile, Twitter is great for sharing quick tips, news, and links to your latest tutorials. Don't forget to leverage LinkedIn to connect with professionals and enthusiasts in the tech industry. Remember, it's not just about broadcasting your content, but also about engaging with your audience, answering questions, and participating in discussions. By actively being part of the community, you can build a strong online presence, increase your credibility, and drive more traffic to your content. Always remember to include call-to-actions in your posts to encourage your audience to read, share, and interact with your content.

Engaging with Your Community: Comments, Feedback, and More

Engaging with your community goes beyond just replying to comments and messages. It's about fostering a dynamic, two-way conversation that builds trust and rapport with your audience. One effective way to do this is by creating a space for your followers to showcase their own Raspberry Pi projects. Invite them to share their creations, challenges faced, and how they overcame them. This not only makes them feel valued, but also provides learning opportunities for the entire community. To further boost engagement, consider running contests, offering prizes for the most innovative projects. This can spur creativity and encourage more people to experiment with Raspberry Pi. Don't forget to highlight and respond to constructive feedback, as this shows you value your audience's input and are committed to improving your content. Remember, a thriving, engaged community is a powerful tool for growth and success in the world of Raspberry Pi entrepreneurship.

Monetizing Content: Ads, Affiliate Marketing, and Sponsorships

One of the viable ways to cash in on your Raspberry Pi content is through ads, affiliate marketing, and sponsorships. Ads, whether banner or video, can generate income based on impressions and clicks. While they can be a source of passive income, make sure they don't interfere with user experience.

Affiliate marketing can also be a lucrative option. If you're recommending Raspberry Pi accessories or related products, joining an affiliate program can earn you a commission on purchases made through your links.

Sponsorships are another avenue worth exploring. If you've built a substantial following, companies may be willing to pay you to promote their products or services. Ensure the sponsor aligns with your audience's interests to maintain authenticity.

Remember, monetization should never compromise the quality of your content or the trust of your audience. Transparency is key — always disclose when posts are sponsored or contain affiliate links. With these strategies, you can turn your passion for Raspberry Pi into a profitable venture.

Collaborations and Guest Appearances

In the dynamic universe of Raspberry Pi, collaborations and guest appearances can significantly expand your horizons, catapulting you into new arenas of innovation and creativity. Teaming up with other Raspberry Pi enthusiasts or experts in your field can not only enhance the quality and diversity of your content but also expose you to their audiences, fueling your growth. Consider partnering for a YouTube tutorial series, a podcast episode, or a co-authored blog post.

Guest appearances are similarly potent. By sharing your expertise on other platforms, you can reach a broader audience, building your reputation and drawing new followers. Look for opportunities to guest on relevant podcasts, write guest articles for established blogs, or participate in panel discussions or webinars.

Remember, the goal of collaborations and guest appearances is not just to increase your visibility, but to share valuable knowledge and insights with the Raspberry Pi community. Be selective about your partnerships, prioritizing those that align with your values and can genuinely benefit your audience. Building a successful Raspberry Pi enterprise isn't a solitary journey; it's a collaborative adventure that thrives on shared passion and collective wisdom.

Continuous Learning and Staying Updated

In the ever-evolving world of Raspberry Pi, staying updated and continuously learning are not just beneficial, they're essential. This isn't a static field, friend. It's a galloping stallion of technological prowess that demands your utmost attention and unceasing curiosity. Make it a hobby, not a chore, to keep up with the latest news, updates, and innovations in this realm. Subscribe to relevant industry blogs, follow key figures in the Raspberry Pi community on social media, and attend conferences or meet-ups whenever possible.

Your drive to learn should be as relentless as an ocean wave, incessantly crashing against the shore. It's through this unquenchable thirst for knowledge that you'll not only keep pace with advancements but also uncover fresh opportunities for growth and diversification. Remember, in the Raspberry Pi universe, not improving is tantamount to moving backwards. Your success in this arena depends on your ability to stay ahead of the curve, absorbing new information, and applying it in innovative and profitable ways. And if you stumble upon a golden nugget of wisdom, don't hoard it. Share it within the community. After all, success is sweeter when savored together.

Future Prospects and Evolving with Technology

The future of Raspberry Pi is as bright as a Las Vegas neon sign, my friend. This pint-sized powerhouse of computing is evolving at a breakneck speed, often outpacing even the most tuned-in tech aficionados. But fear not! This isn't a warning to buckle in for an uncontrollable, wild ride. It's an invitation to soar alongside this meteoric rise in technology. Raspberry Pi's flexibility and adaptability make it capable of handling a multitude of tasks, from running sophisticated home automation systems to driving high-end scientific research. So, don't fret over the intimidating pace of change. Instead, embrace it! Become a part of this exciting journey and let the wave of innovation lift your venture to dizzying heights. Keep refining your skills, continuously adapt your business strategies, and, most importantly, retain a tireless passion for learning. In this thrilling game of technology, the Raspberry Pi isn't just a piece on the board; it's the board itself. And to play well, remember, you're not just following the rules - you're making them.

CHAPTER 16: STRIKING DIGITAL GOLD - MINING CRYPTOCURRENCY WITH RASPBERRY PI

Welcome to the heart of the tech gold rush, partner! If you've been waiting to strike it rich, you're in the right place at the right time. In Chapter 16, we'll be diving deep into the digital rivers to pan for that elusive, intangible gold - Cryptocurrency, using our pocket-sized prospector, the Raspberry Pi. From Bitcoin to Ethereum, the crypto vein runs deep and rich with potential, just waiting for the savvy tech entrepreneur to tap into it. Now, don't get me wrong, this isn't some get-rich-quick scheme. It's a journey into the fascinating world of cryptographic currency, powered by your creativity and augmented by the might of Raspberry Pi. Hold onto your hats, folks. We're about to head into the wild, wild west of the digital frontier.

Gary Covella, Ph.D.

Navigating the Cryptocurrency Landscape: Unearthing the Mechanics of Mining

The concept of cryptocurrency mining can seem as elusive as the digital currencies themselves. Yet, once you dig beneath the surface, it's a straightforward and remarkably captivating process. Cryptocurrency mining is essentially the backbone of the entire crypto ecosystem. It's about validating and recording transactions in a decentralized manner, thereby keeping the crypto network secure and operational. Every time a transaction occurs, it's grouped with others into a 'block'. Miners then solve complex mathematical problems to secure these blocks onto a blockchain, a public ledger of all transactions. In exchange for their efforts, miners are rewarded with new cryptocurrency coins. With the Raspberry Pi, you have the power to participate in this thrilling process, right from the comfort of your own home. So, let's roll up our sleeves, folks! It's time to dive headfirst into the bustling world of cryptocurrency mining.

The Powerhouse Behind the Pixels: Raspberry Pi's Role in Cryptocurrency Mining

First off, let's get one thing straight. Raspberry Pi might be small in size, but don't let that fool you. This tiny computer packs a punch and can effortlessly handle the demanding task of cryptocurrency mining. Key to this is its powerful processor, designed to tackle complex mathematical calculations. It might not outperform larger, more expensive systems, but for its size and cost, it does a stellar job. However, it's not just about power. Raspberry Pi stands out due to its energy efficiency. Mining cryptocurrencies is notorious for consuming vast amounts of electricity. But worry not, with Raspberry Pi, you're stepping into a green, sustainable future. It offers a power-efficient solution without compromising the mining speed or effectiveness. What's more, Raspberry Pi's compatibility with various operating systems and mining software makes it an extremely versatile tool for your mining endeavors. So let's switch on our Raspberry Pis, and let the digital treasure hunt begin!

Gary Covella, Ph.D.

Equip and Embark: Getting Your Raspberry Pi Ready For the Mining Adventure

Before we begin our mining escapade, we need to set up your Raspberry Pi correctly. To get started, you'll need a Raspberry Pi with its power supply, a micro SD card (preferably 8GB or more), and a stable internet connection. You'll also need a USB keyboard, mouse, and a monitor to interact with the system.

Once you've gathered all the essentials, it's time to install the operating system. We recommend using Raspbian, a free operating system based on Debian optimized for the Raspberry Pi's hardware. Raspbian comes with all the programs and tools you need for your mining expedition.

Next up, we need to install a piece of software called a 'miner'. This is the tool that will do the actual mining for us. There are many miners out there, but we'll be using a popular one called 'CPUminer'. It's easy to set up and works well with the Raspberry Pi.

Finally, we need to join a mining pool. This is a group of miners who combine their computational power to increase the chances of mining a block. When the pool successfully mines a block, the reward is split amongst the pool members. A mining pool is a great way for small miners like us to earn a steady stream of income.

And with that, you're all set to begin mining with your Raspberry Pi! Remember, mining takes time and patience, but with a little bit of luck and a lot of persistence, you could be on your way to amassing your digital fortune.

Picking the Ideal Cryptocurrency: Align Your Raspberry Pi's Capabilities with Profit Potential

The cryptocurrency market is as diverse as it is dynamic, with thousands of options available. Not all cryptocurrencies, however, are cut from the same cloth. Some require more computational power to mine than others, and therefore may not be compatible with the Raspberry Pi's modest capabilities. For instance, mining Bitcoin would be like trying to win a drag race with a moped - futile and frustrating. Instead, you should focus on cryptocurrencies that are within your Raspberry Pi's reach. Coins like Litecoin, Dogecoin, or the privacy-centric Monero are more suitable candidates. These coins still require processing power to mine, but they are realistically within the grasp of a Raspberry Pi.

But it's not just about picking a coin that your Raspberry Pi can handle. You also need to consider the profitability of the coin. Factors such as the coin's market value, its mining difficulty, and the competition among miners all impact potential earnings. Additionally, consider the coin's utility and future prospects. Is it widely accepted for transactions? Does it have a unique feature that could drive demand in the future? These are all important questions to consider when choosing a cryptocurrency to mine with your Raspberry Pi. Choose wisely, and your tiny computer could become a profitable micro mining rig.

Choosing the Right Mining Software

After you've zeroed in on the ideal cryptocurrency to mine on your Raspberry

Pi Profits

Pi, the next step is selecting the appropriate mining software. Just as the cryptocurrency world is diverse, so is the realm of mining software. There's a vast array of options available, each with its own unique features and strengths. Your choice of software should align with your chosen cryptocurrency, your Raspberry Pi's capabilities, and your personal requirements.

Some popular mining software options compatible with Raspberry Pi include CGMiner and EasyMiner. CGMiner is a versatile option, known for its adaptability with a range of hardware, and its compatibility with most types of cryptocurrencies. Its interface may seem intimidating to beginners, but it offers a wealth of advanced features for seasoned miners. EasyMiner, on the other hand, is perfect for novices stepping into the world of crypto mining. It sports a user-friendly graphical interface and supports a variety of cryptocurrencies.

Remember, the right software can significantly influence your mining success. It serves as your primary tool for cryptocurrency extraction, so ensure it's not just compatible with your hardware and chosen cryptocurrency, but also user-friendly and equipped with the necessary features to optimize your mining operations.

Amplifying Your Mining Success: The Power of Mining Pools

Mining pools are the secret sauce to amplifying your cryptocurrency mining success. When you dive into the complex world of crypto, you quickly realize mining solo can feel like trying to find a needle in a haystack. This is where mining pools come into play.

Think of mining pools as a lottery syndicate. By pooling your resources with other miners, you're betting on the increased odds of finding that valuable block of cryptocurrency. Instead of going it alone and hoping for a big win, you're part of a group that shares the rewards proportional to the amount of computational power each member contributes.

Some popular mining pools include Slush Pool for Bitcoin miners and NanoPool which supports a range of cryptocurrencies. Joining a mining pool is straightforward, simply sign up on their website, configure your mining software with the pool's information, and you're set to start mining. But remember, most pools charge a fee for their services, typically a small percentage of your mining rewards, so factor this into your calculations when deciding whether to join a pool.

Mining pools can certainly boost your chances of success in the cryptocurrency game. The combined power of numerous Raspberry Pi machines working in unison can prove quite a force in the crypto mining world. So, while the lone wolf miner can still strike gold, think of mining pools as your trusty companions in this digital gold rush.

Unleashing the Power: Amplifying Your Raspberry Pi Mining Efficiency

Optimizing your Raspberry Pi for mining is no less than an art. It's a fine balance between efficiency and performance, ensuring your micro-machine runs smoothly while crunching those complex calculations. Start with a lean operating system; Raspbian Lite is a great choice, offering the necessary functionality without any unnecessary frills.

Next, overclock your Raspberry Pi. Squeezing every bit of computational power from your Pi can significantly enhance your mining results. But tread lightly! Overclocking can lead to overheating, so ensure you have a robust cooling system in place.

Thirdly, consider using mining-specific software like CGMiner or BFGMiner. These are designed to maximize your hashing rate, speeding up the discovery of new blocks.

Finally, keep your software up-to-date. New releases often provide performance improvements and security patches. Ongoing optimization is key to successful and profitable mining. With the right approach, your Raspberry Pi can be a force to reckon with in the crypto mining world.

Assessing the Potential: Profits, Perils, and Projections

When diving into the world of crypto mining with your Raspberry Pi, it's crucial to understand not just the potential for profit, but also the inherent risks and challenges. Crypto mining isn't a guaranteed goldmine—it's a volatile landscape, where the value of your mined currency can fluctuate wildly. It's not just about the initial setup. Your electricity costs, the efficiency of your mining rig, and the current market rate for the cryptocurrency you're mining all play a significant role in determining your profitability.

Crypto mining is also competitive. As more people enter the arena, the difficulty of solving the complex calculations necessary to mine cryptocurrency increases. This, in turn, requires more powerful and efficient hardware. As a miner, you'll always be in a race to stay ahead of the curve, continually optimizing your setup to maintain profitability.

Risks aren't just confined to the market either. Overclocking your Raspberry Pi can lead to overheating and, in extreme cases, hardware failure. Security is another concern. Keeping your software up-to-date is absolutely essential to protect yourself from hackers and malware.

However, with risk comes reward. Despite the challenges, crypto mining can be lucrative, particularly if you're able to optimize your mining rig and navigate the market effectively. It's a robust, engaging foray into the world of digital currency—and your Raspberry Pi is your ticket in. Keep your expectations realistic, stay informed about the market, and always be ready to learn and adapt.

Navigating the Cryptocurrency Mining Landscape: Ensuring Optimal Performance of Your Raspberry Pi

Maintaining a Raspberry Pi mining operation requires meticulous care, frequent check-ups, and regular updates. Keeping your Raspberry Pi functioning optimally is paramount to your mining success. Here's a handy tip: regulate the temperature of your device. Overheating can lead to hardware damage or even failure, so consider investing in a cooling system or heat sinks. Frequent system checks and updates are not just preventative measures against overheating, they are critical for your device's security. Cyber threats are an ever-present danger in the crypto world, with malware and hackers always on the prowl. Regular software updates help patch any vulnerabilities and enhance your Raspberry Pi's immunity against such threats. Additionally, ensure you have a reliable power supply. Unexpected shutdowns due to power failures can cause data loss or hardware damage. Lastly, stay informed and adaptable. The crypto mining landscape is dynamic and constantly evolving. Keep abreast with the latest trends, technologies and market conditions. Remember, your Raspberry Pi is a powerful tool, but its performance ultimately depends on how well you maintain and operate it.

Delving Into the Legalities and Ethics of Cryptocurrency Mining

When embarking on a journey into the realm of cryptocurrency mining, one cannot ignore the legal and ethical considerations that come along with it. From a legal standpoint, the status and regulations of cryptocurrency mining vary significantly from country to

Gary Covella, Ph.D.

country. While some nations have embraced this digital revolution, others have imposed restrictions or outright bans. Therefore, it's crucial for miners to familiarize themselves with the local laws and regulations pertaining to cryptocurrency to avoid potential legal repercussions.

Similarly, venturing into crypto mining raises ethical questions. The vast energy consumption associated with mining operations has often been criticized due to its environmental impact. Therefore, miners should consider seeking out and utilizing renewable or more energy-efficient methods to lessen their carbon footprint. Furthermore, it's essential to maintain transparency and honesty when conducting mining operations. Given the anonymous nature of cryptocurrency, it's unfortunately been used in illegal activities like money laundering. Therefore, miners must ensure their operations respect and uphold ethical standards and contribute positively to the crypto community.

Remember, with great power (or in this case, great computational power) comes great responsibility. Strive to be a

304.

responsible and ethical miner in the digital gold rush era of cryptocurrency.

How to Profit from Cryptocurrency Mining

Step 1: Education and Research

Your first step should be to understand exactly how mining works. Educate yourself about the intricacies of cryptocurrencies, blockchain technology, mining processes, and the market trends. Familiarize yourself with the legal and ethical aspects to ensure your mining operations are legitimate and environmentally friendly. Remember, knowledge is your most valuable asset.

Step 2: Choose Your Cryptocurrency

Choose which cryptocurrency you want to mine. Bitcoin is the most well-known, but there are others like Ethereum, Litecoin, and more. Each has its own advantages, challenges, and profitability. Your decision will significantly impact your mining operations.

Gary Covella, Ph.D.

Step 3: Invest in Hardware and Software

Depending on your cryptocurrency of choice, you may need to invest in hardware like a GPU (Graphics Processing Unit) or ASIC (Application-Specific Integrated Circuit) miners. Remember, the better the hardware, the more effectively you can mine. You'll also need to choose appropriate mining software to manage your mining operations.

Step 4: Join a Mining Pool

Considering the competition in mining, you might want to join a mining pool. This is a group of miners who come together to pool their computational power and share the mined cryptocurrency. This way, even if you don't solve the complex problem first, you'll still get a share of the profit.

Step 5: Start Mining

Once you've set everything up, you can start mining. Keep a close eye on your operations, market trends, and energy consumption. As you become more adept, adjust your mining strategies to maximize profits.

Pi Profits

Step 6: Regularly Convert Cryptocurrency into Fiat Currency

To profit from your mining operations, regularly convert your mined cryptocurrency into fiat currency. However, be strategic about this. Keep an eye on the market and sell when rates are favorable.

Step 7: Reinvest Profits Wisely

Use your profits to scale your operation by investing in better hardware or diving into other cryptocurrencies.

Remember, cryptocurrency mining is a marathon, not a sprint. It requires patience, strategy, and continuous learning. Keep pushing forward, and the digital gold rush could pay off handsomely.

To further your knowledge and stay up-to-date with the latest mining trends, consider these resources:

Bitcoin.org: This is the official site for Bitcoin and a great starting point for beginners. Here, you'll find everything you need to know about Bitcoin and mining, FAQs, and a discussion forum.

307.

Gary Covella, Ph.D.

CoinDesk: CoinDesk provides the latest news on cryptocurrencies and blockchain technology. The site also has a dedicated section for learning about Bitcoin.

CryptoCompare: This is an interactive platform where you can discuss the latest trends, monitor live streaming prices, review and compare crypto assets.

Reddit Cryptocurrency: Reddit's cryptocurrency community is a valuable resource for asking questions and engaging in discussions about all things crypto. Be sure to check out their Mining section.

Cryptocurrency Mining vs. Bitcoin Mining Profitability: This tool allows you to compare the profitability of mining different cryptocurrencies.

Remember, the world of cryptocurrency mining is constantly evolving. So, keep learning and stay informed.

CONCLUSION: THE BOUNDLESS FRONTIER OF MICRO-MACHINE POSSIBILITIES

As we stand on the precipice of a new age, where technology and ambition intertwine to build a brighter future, it's clear that the power within your grasp is extraordinary, thanks to this tiny titan of a computer. From art installations flashing with synchronized LEDs to intricate tech systems revamping agriculture, opportunities abound.

Whether you're an educator illuminating young minds, an artist painting with digital brushes, or a techie coding the future, this compact computer is your gateway to a brave new world. The entrepreneurial landscape is vast, and with this micro-machine, you're equipped to navigate the ever-evolving terrain.

Gary Covella, Ph.D.

In this book, we've unearthed strategies, traced diverse ventures, and explored the multitude of applications this potent technology offers. We've walked a path, not just of learning, but of envisioning, innovating, and transforming ideas into tangible, profitable realities.

Never forget that this journey into the realm of micro-computing isn't a sprint; it's a marathon, demanding patience, resilience, and an unquenchable thirst for knowledge. Cryptocurrency mining, creating gaming consoles, automating homes; each chapter was a testament to the transformative power of this micro-machine.

Remember, just as the world of cryptocurrency mining is ceaselessly progressing, so too is the world of micro-computing. Stay curious, keep learning, and fuel your passion to innovate. The frontier is boundless, and the only limit is the sky.

Let this book serve not just as a comprehensive guide but as a launching pad, propelling you into a world pregnant with possibilities. Dive into the digital gold rush and make your mark. Venture forth, pioneers of the new

310.

Pi Profits

age, and let the era of micro-machine
supremacy begin.